M000163758

Daily Lent Reflections

Nick Fawcett

kevin
mayhew

First published in 2003 by

KEVIN MAYHEW LTD
Buxhall, Stowmarket, Suffolk, IP14 3BW
E-mail: info@kevinmayhewltd.com

KINGSGATE PUBLISHING INC
1000 Pannell Street, Suite G, Columbia, MO 65201
E-mail: sales@kingsgatepublishing.com

9 8 7 6 5 4 3 2 1

ISBN 1 84417 176 0
Catalogue No 1500665

Cover design by Jo Balaam
Edited by Katherine Laidler
Typesetting by Fiona Connell Finch
Printed in Great Britain

Contents

Introduction

In what ways do you observe Lent? Indeed, do you observe it at all? Many feel that they ought to do something special during this season but are unsure quite what that something should be. Others follow the traditional practices of discipline and self-denial, perhaps seeking to conquer a particular failing, perhaps denying themselves certain pleasures or luxuries, or perhaps setting aside time for fasting. These have their time-honoured place but by themselves they don't necessarily deepen our devotional life. We need something more if we are to do that: a focus for our thoughts; what we might term spiritual food to nurture our faith and discipleship.

In this book I have attempted to provide just that or, rather, to make more accessible the spiritual sustenance already offered by Jesus in what must surely be some of his best-known and best-loved words: the Sermon on the Mount, recorded in Matthew, chapters 5 to 7. Reading and rereading those chapters, 40 topics suggested themselves for further reflection, one for each day of Lent. Many are interrelated; the more you study the 'sermon', the more apparent the interweaving of its underlying key themes becomes: themes such as forgiving others, doing that little bit extra in God's service, choosing the way of the kingdom instead of the often-enticing 'way of the world', seeking God's will rather than our own, valuing and respecting others. How do we work out such ideas in terms of daily life? What are their implications for you and me today? Those are the kind of questions I have set out to answer in this book. My aim is not in any sense to provide additional wisdom or advice of my own, but simply to bring home the challenge, promise, encouragement and inspiration implicit within the teaching of Jesus, teaching that must surely provide the clearest blueprint for Christian living in all the Bible. If we hear and focus more clearly upon what *he* has to say, then this season of Lent will be special indeed!

NICK FAWCETT

5

In tribute to my aunt, Hazel Fawcett,
who has displayed such faith and
courage across the years

Day 1: Blessing for the poor in spirit

Approach

Gracious God,
   I come as I am,
   in all my weakness,
   with all my faults,
   seeking your renewing, restoring touch.
Reach out in love,
   receive me by your grace,
   and work in me through your Spirit,
   to your glory.
Amen.

Read

Blessed are those who are poor in spirit; to them belongs the kingdom of heaven.
Matthew 5:3

Reflect

Few passages of Scripture are better loved than the Beatitudes, yet probably few are less well understood. The verses have an innate beauty, a poetry about them that appeals to something deep within, but what does it actually mean to be pure in heart, meek, or, above all, poor in spirit? Poverty of any sort is not something we naturally aspire to, and to be poor in terms of material possessions is certainly not what most of us would term a blessing. There can surely be few more painful experiences than to have nothing and be totally dependent on the charity of others. Yet, in terms of our relationship with God, we are all in precisely that position, if we did but know it. None of us deserves his goodness; no one can earn his blessing; nobody can merit his love. We come before God spiritually bankrupt, reliant upon his generosity; his willingness to give and go on giving despite rather than because of our efforts. Recognise that emptiness, however, and God is able to fill us. Accept our need and he will respond. Happy indeed, then, are those who are truly poor in spirit, for their lives are fully opened to the rich blessings of his kingdom that God waits to shower upon them, both now and for all eternity.

Pray

Me?
Poor in spirit?
I'd like to think so, Lord,
    but I'm not, am I? –
    not by a long chalk.
Poor in faith, perhaps;
    in commitment,
    worship,
    service;
    but in terms of spirit it's an altogether different story.
I'm full of myself, truth be told,
    not in the sense of pride –
    or at least I hope not –
    but in the sense of self-will,
    self-centredness,
    self-indulgence,
    constantly putting *my* interests before yours,
    my goals,
    my dreams,
    my wishes
    before *your* purpose.
It's human, of course –
    you know that as much as any –
    but though you continue to reach out regardless,
    arms outstretched in love,
    I unwittingly rebuff your embrace,

8

turning aside,
backing away,
forever keeping you at a distance.
Forgive me, Lord,
and help me to change.
Teach me to value myself, as you do,
but, above all, to value you
and the things of your kingdom.
Teach me to stand tall as your child,
but also to humble myself under your mighty hand,
and so in my need may I find succour,
and in my poverty, riches beyond measure.
Amen.

Ponder

- Do you recognise your total dependence on God's grace, or do you still try to earn his blessing?
- In what other ways, apart from receiving forgiveness, are you finally dependent on God?
- Does your life find its ultimate meaning in God or in something or someone else?

Close

Loving God,
send me on my way
conscious not just of my dependence on you
but also of your faithfulness in meeting my need,
constantly and graciously reaching out in mercy
to forgive and bless.
May that knowledge colour every moment
and give meaning to every day,
through Jesus Christ my Lord.
Amen.

Day 2: Blessing for those who mourn

Approach

God of all comfort,
   in the traumas and tragedies of life,
   the vagaries of our ever-changing world,
   speak your word,
   grant your strength
   and minister your love,
   through Jesus Christ my Lord.
Amen.

Read

Blessed are those who mourn, for they will receive comfort.
Matthew 5:4

Reflect

If there is one line of Scripture that sums up God's promise of comfort for those who mourn it is surely the opening line of Psalm 23, immortalised in the hymn by Francis Rous 'The Lord's my shepherd, I'll not want', set, of course, to the tune *Crimond*. The words have touched a chord with successive generations as few others have even begun to, such that the twenty-third psalm is probably one of the few passages of Scripture that the average person in the street will recognise. So what is the reason for this hymn's popularity? Is it simply tradition, the fact that across the years the hymn has been sung at countless funeral services up and down the country? Is it that the tune has some special attraction? Or is it that people are moved by the poetry of the words and the sentiments behind them: the idea of a divine being watching over us, both in life and death, as attentively as a shepherd in ancient Israel would have looked after his flock? All these might offer some explanation, but there is, I believe, one reason that out-weighs any other: simply the fact that many have found the words of the Psalm to be true in their own experience. God, they have learned, does indeed watch over us, his hand always there to lead, restore, strengthen and bless, and, in times of sorrow, to support and comfort. Even in the trauma of bereavement, the heartbreak of loss, he is able to bring consolation – not in the shape of pious platitudes or easy answers, but drawing alongside us, sharing our pain, and offering the promise of life beyond death, hope beyond the grave.

Christians, like anyone else, will experience their fair share of tragedy and sadness, moments when life seems bleak beyond redemption and joy appears consigned to the past, yet repeatedly in Scripture we are reminded that, as Jesus declared in the Sermon on the Mount, those who mourn will be comforted. 'When my heart is filled by cares too many to number,' writes the Psalmist (Psalm 94:19), 'you bring comfort and cheer to my soul.' 'Glory to the God and Father of our Lord Jesus Christ,' writes Paul in his second letter to the Corinthians (1:3-6), 'the Father of compassion and God of all consolation, who comforts us in times of trouble so that we might comfort others wrestling with similar burdens with the comfort that God has granted us. Just as the agonies of Christ are numerous for us, so also we receive copious consolation through Christ.' Similarly, Paul writes once again, this time to the Thessalonians (2 Thessalonians 2:16-17), 'May our Lord Jesus Christ and God our Father, who loved us and through grace gave us everlasting comfort and a certain hope, give comfort to your hearts, building them up in all good words and deeds.' Here is the God we worship at Advent; the God who has come to us in Christ, sharing our humanity, enduring pain, tasting sorrow and facing death itself to bring us life. Here is the God who has given his all so that, whatever we might face, we have the assur-ance of his comfort. 'The Lord's my shepherd, I'll not want . . .

11

Even though I walk through the darkest of valleys, I fear no evil, for you are with me, your rod and staff a constant source of comfort.' Trust in that promise; it will not fail.

Pray

I don't know how I'll cope, Lord,
    I really don't.
When tragedy strikes,
    as one day it unquestionably will,
    I'm not sure how I'll take it;
    whether I'll have the strength I need,
    the inner resources,
    to keep my head above water,
    or whether I'll sink like a stone,
    overwhelmed by the trauma,
    engulfed by grief,
    drowning in despair.
I hope I'll be strong,
    but even the *thought* of calamity sets my hairs on end,
    never mind the reality.
I dread the aching sense of loss,
    the pall of sorrow,
    the utter brokenness of heart and spirit,
    those themselves too much to bear,
    but I fear also the simplistic words of consolation some
        will offer,
    sincere enough,
    well-intended,
    yet promising peace where there is no peace,
    cheer where there is no cheer,
    and answers where there is only confusion.
Remind me, Lord, of your assurance
    that those who mourn shall be comforted,
    that tears will give way to laughter
    and that light will triumph over darkness.

Remind me that whatever I face, I will not be alone;
    that in the shadow of sorrow
    and the valley of death
    you will be there.
And remind me, also, of all those across the years
    who have discovered the same,
    finding in you not just one to share their pain
    but one who also leads them through it to new beginnings,
    a new dawn.
Would I cope, Lord?
I just don't know,
    but thankfully even if *I* fail,
    you won't,
    your love unfailing,
    your promise true,
    your comfort assured.
Receive my praise,
    in Jesus' name.
Amen.

Ponder

- Have experiences of grief and tragedy left scars in your life that continue to cause you pain? Have you brought those experiences to God in prayer, opening up to him about how you are feeling?
- Have there been times when you have found comfort through faith? What were these, and how did faith help you get through them?
- Are there ways in which experiences of sorrow have helped shape you positively as a person? In what way might we use such experiences for good?

Close

Compassionate God,
    reach out into the sorrows, hurt, disappointments and regrets
    that I carry within me,
    and grant the comfort that you alone can bring.
Wipe away the tears,
    tend the wounds
    and mend the brokenness of body, mind and spirit,
    through Jesus Christ my Lord.
Amen.

Day 3: Blessing for the meek

Approach

Loving God,
    I come seeking not my will but yours,
    not my way but your kingdom,
    not my interests but your glory.
Meet with me in these moments I've set aside
    for worship and reflection,
    so that I may offer you more faithfully
    the discipleship I yearn to give,
    through Jesus Christ my Lord.
Amen.

Read

Blessed are the meek, for they will inherit the earth.
Matthew 5:5 (NRSV)

Reflect

Ask people what characteristic they would most like to be recognised for, and you can be fairly sure that meekness would not feature high on their list. More likely, if it appeared at all, it would come bottom; the word, as we understand it today, typically associated with timidity, nervousness, diffidence; a willingness to be put upon, taken advantage of, treated like a doormat, enduring whatever is thrown at us with barely a whimper. Who wants to be a person like that, and which among us would see such a disposition as the hallmark of a Christian? For many, then, these words of Jesus present something of a problem, for they seem to confirm our worst fears, idealising the wishy-washy picture most people have of Christians as somewhat soppy if well-meaning. That, however, is categorically not what Jesus had in mind when he spoke of the meek. His words, like those concerning the poor in spirit, apply solely to our relationship with God, and denote a readiness to subjugate our will to his purpose, to accept his guidance and authority and to defer to his wishes. Is that what typifies our discipleship? Admittedly, it's difficult sometimes to know what his will in a particular situation might be, but do we even seek it or do we prefer instead to pursue our own way? Do we measure our lifestyle, our thoughts, words and deeds, against the teaching God has given in Scripture and the example he has shown in Christ, or do we simply pay him lip service, professing one thing but doing another? There is nothing weak or timid about true meekness – indeed, it may prove to be just the opposite, showing itself, for example, in a willingness to make a stand for what we believe in, speaking out perhaps to challenge injustice and confront evil, or in acts of courage and self-sacrifice, or in a commitment to bold initiatives, or in numerous other ways; doing, in other words, whatever it is we believe God is asking of us. Do we exhibit such obedience in our relationship with God, or are we swift to rebel when his will conflicts with our own, stubbornly asserting our wishes against his? We may secure short-term satisfaction through the latter, but ultimately at the cost of our eternal inheritance, for in losing touch with God we will lose sight also of his kingdom, both here on earth as well as in heaven.

Pray

Lord,
    save me from meekness as the world sees it:
    from a spirit of timidity and indecision,
    an attitude of compliance and cowardice,
    a character perceived as spineless,
    submissive,
    subservient.
Grant me, instead, true meekness:
    a willingness to trust in your purpose and obey your commands,
    to respond to your guidance and step out in faith.

Isn't that what discipleship should mean:
    being ready to speak out against wrong and stand up against evil,
    to take on a challenge and venture into the unknown,
    meeting obstacles, difficulties and disappointments,
    yet, if it is your will,
    persevering to the end,
    risking all if necessary?
I don't want to be a caricature, Lord,
    the sort of person who confirms the view most people have
    of Christians and the Church,
    and I don't believe you want that either,
    so my prayer today is simply this:
    grant me meekness,
    not weakness!
Amen.

Ponder

- Have you sometimes confused weakness and meekness? Which of the two characterises your discipleship?
- What image do you think people have of Christians? Why do they hold this? Is it justified?
- Is there an area in your life where God is calling you to put him first and yourself second?

Close

Sovereign God,
    whenever you speak, teach me to listen;
    whatever you ask, teach me to respond;
    wherever you lead, teach me to follow;
    however you work, teach me to trust.
Give me a spirit of true meekness,
    ready to give you pride of place in my life
    and to offer you obedient and devoted service,
    through Jesus Christ my Lord.
Amen.

17

Day 4: Blessing for those who yearn for righteousness

Approach

Loving God,
 awaken in me a hunger to know you more deeply,
 a yearning to grow in faith
 and a longing to serve you better.
Show me my need
 and the way you alone can meet it,
 through Christ my Lord.
Amen.

Read

Blessed are those who are hungry and thirsty for righteousness;
they will be satisfied.
Matthew 5:6

Reflect

'Mum,' said the child to his mother as they queued at the supermarket checkout, 'I'm hungry.' He wasn't really, of course, or at least not especially so, but he'd spotted the display of sweets strategically placed there for just such a moment. In reality, that 'hunger' was merely a passing fancy. The little boy would have enjoyed a chocolate bar no doubt, but had the mother succumbed to his wishes, what are the chances, I wonder, that he would have tucked into his next meal? As any nutritionist will tell you, junk food is one of the great health problems of our time, many of our young people – and some not so young – prejudicing their long-term health through an unhealthy and unbalanced diet.

The parallels between this and hungering and thirsting after righteousness are obvious. Few of us have any real idea what hunger is, either physically or spiritually. We may have experienced a rumbling stomach on the odd occasion, even perhaps have missed the isolated meal or fasted for a day or two, but when you compare that with the starving millions of our world, it quickly pales into insignificance. To crave not so much our next meal but simply a morsel to eat is simply beyond our experience, yet that's the sort of hunger God wants us to show for spiritual things: a deep, urgent yearning to know more of him and to serve him better. Instead, most of the time, we are content to dip in as the mood takes us, fitting in a devotional titbit here, a morsel of prayer there, and so on.

We *do*, though, hunger for certain things, or at least we find it hard not to: the trappings of success – money, possessions and the like – and we fill ourselves with junk food of a different kind, cramming our days with so much that is insubstantial, unable, ultimately, truly to satisfy. The result, of course, is spiritual emaciation, stunted growth as Christians, yet too often we fail to see the link, wondering why our faith seems frail and our spiritual requirements remain unsatiated.

We need, while celebrating this world God has given us and savouring his precious gift of life, to hunger and thirst also for what really matters: for bread of life and living water; for the sustenance that Christ alone can give – food for our souls.

Pray

Lord,
    I don't know what it is to be hungry . . .
    really hungry . . .
    for I'm one of the world's lucky ones,
    having more than enough food to eat every day.
The most I get is peckish,
    relishing the thought of a good meal,
    but that's enough for me to recognise
    that I rarely hunger either for spiritual things,
    let alone thirst after righteousness.

I may have done once,
    yearning for something to give shape and direction to my life,
    and perhaps in the early days,
    the first flush of commitment,
    I *was* eager,
    devouring your word expectantly,
    aching to feast more deeply in times of prayer and worship.
But that's all a memory now,
    a dim recollection,
    the reality today so very different.
Far from craving nourishment
    I take the occasional snack,
    the odd nibble,
    the isolated sip,
    feeding on your word as the inclination takes me,
    dipping into desultory acts of devotion,
    snatching a quick dose of prayer in times of crisis . . .
    and that's about it.
No wonder I struggle, Lord,
    my faith fragile,
    my discipleship weak,
    for that's no kind of diet,
    hardly enough even to sustain life
    let alone encourage growth.
Forgive me,
    and create in me, through your Spirit,
    a genuine and passionate desire
    for the things of your kingdom:
    a hankering truly to love you,
    a longing to contribute more fully in your service,
    an unquenchable appetite to reach maturity in Christ.
I've not been hungry, Lord,
    nor thirsted as I should,
    but at least now I see it
    and realise how empty I am.

Come, then,
    keep hunger alive,
    and, in your mercy, satisfy me,
    body and soul,
    day by day.
Amen.

Ponder

- Do you still hunger and thirst to know God better?
- With what do you feed and nurture your faith?
- What does the quality of your daily discipleship say about your spiritual diet and appetite for the things of God? Does it accord with the answer you gave to the first question above?

Close

Sovereign God,
    I have tasted your goodness,
    experienced your love,
    sampled the new life you have won for me in Christ,
    and I hunger to feed more fully
    and drink more deeply.
Fill me now by your Spirit
    with the bread of life
    and streams of living water,
    and so may I find nourishment for my soul,
    through Jesus Christ my Lord.
Amen.

Day 5: Blessing for the merciful

Approach

Gracious God,
  I draw near to you,
  trusting not in any goodness of my own
  but in your grace,
  your love,
  your unfailing, overflowing mercy.
Open my heart to all you would say
  and my life to all you would do
  by your grace
  and to your glory.
Amen.

Read

Blessed are those who show mercy; they will receive mercy in turn.
Matthew 5:7

Reflect

When you read the Beatitudes, whom do you think Jesus is talking about? Do you see the poor in spirit and pure in heart, the meek and those who hunger and thirst after righteous as some special saintly breed of person, or as applying, at least potentially, to you? I don't think I've ever seriously considered that question before, but, as I read the Beatitudes again while writing this book, it struck me as never before that Jesus wants us to show such qualities in our lives. Nowhere is that more so than with the words 'Blessed are those who show mercy'. Jesus returns to this theme at several points during the Sermon on the Mount, so the idea is clearly central to his teaching. He doesn't just want us to admire the merciful but to show mercy ourselves; in other words, to forgive others as God has forgiven us. Nothing too hard about that, we might think, but we'd be wrong, for displaying true mercy is one of the hardest things there is. Our gut reaction when we are hurt is to want to hurt back. The norm when we are wronged is to seek recompense or revenge. And when someone lets us down – especially if they do so badly or repeatedly – we find it difficult, if not impossible, fully to trust that person again.

As Christians we may succeed in overcoming our natural instincts sufficiently to avoid the first two responses, but the third is a tougher nut to crack. We may *say* we forgive someone, we may even believe we have, but truly to do so is a different matter. All too often, in times of conflict or anger, we dredge up old mistakes, using what ostensibly we've forgiven as ammunition to snipe and wound. The poison of unresolved hurt and unforgiven mistakes – real or otherwise – is still there, eating away within, waiting to be spat out when the opportunity presents itself. Such feelings are not only hugely destructive of our relationships but also of us as individuals, for, imperceptibly, they nibble away at the fruits of Christian discipleship – love, joy, peace, gentleness, kindness – replacing them with a mean, bitter and carping disposition. If we do not forgive others, we slowly become estranged from them. Worse still, we estrange ourselves from God, the burden of resentment and hurt impeding us from responding to his love, tying us down to our own small world. Don't let that happen to you. Forgive as you have been forgiven, as you *would* be forgiven. 'Blessed are those who show mercy; they will receive mercy in turn.'

Pray

I should have forgiven, Lord –
    put the issue behind us and started again –
    but I hadn't . . .
    I still haven't . . .
    and we're all paying the price.

I was hurt, that's the trouble –
    hurt, bitter and angry –
    and I wanted not only my pain acknowledged
    but also some assurance that it wouldn't happen again,
    that the words of apology were sincere,
    actually meaning something,
    rather than a hollow platitude,
    designed merely to retain the peace.
So I kept it going–
    scowling,
    stewing,
    sulking;
    forever brooding on the perceived injustice,
    magnifying it out of all proportion
    until it dominated every thought,
    every word,
    every deed.
I meant to hurt back, I suppose,
    to give a taste of how I felt,
    and I'm ashamed to say I've succeeded in that all too well.
But I've hurt myself just as much,
    and others too,
    the toxin of resentment infecting my very being,
    festering deep within,
    poisoning my relationships with all.
Forgive me, Lord,
    and, by your grace,
    replace the cinders of resentment, umbrage and self-pity
    with the fire of love,
    and so may I not just receive your blessing
    but also impart it to others,
    through Jesus Christ my Lord.
Amen.

Ponder

- Do you harbour a grudge or grievance against anyone? Isn't it time you let go?
- When embroiled in an argument, do you bring up past mistakes? Are you being fair? Again, isn't it time you put the past to bed?
- What do you find hardest about forgiving? Is it really possible to forgive and forget?

Close

Gracious God,
> teach me not just to talk of forgiveness
> but also truly to show it:
> abandoning resentment,
> blotting out past mistakes,
> forgetting they ever happened,
> and offering a new beginning,
> the opportunity to start again.

As you have done for me,
> teach me to do for others,
> in Jesus' name.

Amen.

Day 6: Blessing for the pure in heart

Approach

Living God,
   speak to me afresh,
   so that I might know you more fully,
   love you more deeply
   and serve you more richly,
   to the glory of your name.
Amen.

Read

Blessed are the pure in heart, for they will see God.
Matthew 5:8 (NRSV)

Reflect

'Pure': it's a word we hear bandied about in all sorts of contexts, isn't it? 'Pure genius' says a recent advert for a well-known brand of beer. 'Pure gold' was the claim made for a building society investment account. Pure, clear, fresh is the pitch chosen by marketing people for such products as soap, fruit juice and mineral water. The word may be overplayed, but the way it is used is instructive in relation to the words of Jesus, 'Blessed are the pure in heart', for they remind us that Jesus had in mind something much larger than simply moral purity. That's how some tend to interpret this saying, and they are right in part, for certainly avoiding what we might call improper thoughts is part of what he was getting at, but the primary meaning of 'purity' – and the one exploited in advertising – is the idea of being unadulterated, unsullied, all of a kind; nothing added and nothing taken away; 100 per cent what it claims to be.

It's not hard to see how all this might relate to Christian disciple-ship. Purity, understood thus, asks searching questions concerning our thoughts and attitudes, our innermost motives for acting, thinking and speaking as we do. Is who and what we are in tune with God, totally at one with his will? Or are our words and deeds tarnished by greed, envy, lust, bitterness, pride? Are we 100-percent committed to God so that we strive in every aspect of our lives to honour him? That's what it means to be pure in heart, its significance extending far wider than any narrow understanding of moral purity.

I doubt anyone comes remotely near that ideal, but it offers us a goal to strive towards, one encapsulated in the words of Jesus, 'Be perfect, as your heavenly Father is perfect.' Unrealistic? Out of the question? In this life, of course it is, but it is nonetheless a target to aim for. The more we attain such purity of heart, such undivided, undiluted commitment, the more we will indeed see God, for we will be one with him and he one with us.

Pray

I thought I was getting close, Lord;
    that at least, if not controlling them entirely,
    I was on top of my unworthy thoughts,
    able to nip them in the bud
    before they fully took hold.
It may not sound much,
    but for me it was an achievement,
    for it doesn't come easily, such discipline,
    lust, greed, deceit and envy being too much a part of me –
    hard to resist, easy to excuse.
I've avoided those, Lord –
    most of the time, anyway –
    my thoughts turned, as far as I could make them,
    on what is good,
    pleasing,
    true,
    honouring to you.

Yet while that, if only in part, is purity of *mind*,
>it's not purity of *heart*,
>for it's been a daily struggle,
>an uphill battle to conquer my inclinations
>and control my impulses,
>to be what I wish I could be
>rather than what I am.
It's a start, isn't it,
>but I'll never achieve that goal in my own strength,
>only through your grace.
So draw me closer, Lord,
>and, in your love, work within me.
Wash me,
>and I shall be whiter than snow.
Touch me,
>and I shall be clean.
Put a new heart and a right spirit within me,
>so that I may delight to do your will
>and yearn to honour you always.
Take what I am,
>and direct what I shall be,
>through Jesus Christ my Lord.
Amen.

Ponder

- How would you describe impure thoughts? Do these still have a hold in your life?
- Do you understand these words of Jesus simply in terms of morality? Have you ever considered what he might be saying more widely concerning the quality and integrity of your discipleship?
- Do you attempt to achieve purity of heart through striving to live better or through cultivating your relationship with God?

Close

Living God,
    cleanse me of all that is unworthy,
    rid me of all that is false,
    redeem me from all that is wrong.
Grant me a pure heart
    and a right spirit,
    by the grace of Christ,
    my Lord and Saviour.
Amen.

Day 7: Blessing for the peacemakers

Approach

Loving God,
  reach out to me and fill me with your peace,
  so that, in turn, I might reach out to others,
  and by your grace be a means
  through which you work for harmony and reconciliation.
In the name of Christ, I ask it.
Amen.

Read

Blessed are the peacemakers, for God will call them his children.
Matthew 5:9

Reflect

What does it mean to be a peacemaker and what qualities are needed to fulfil that role? Some might see it as getting the parties to a dispute simply to co-exist, but that's not necessarily the same thing as peace, not if past resentments, suspicions and hostilities are simmering beneath the surface. Others might feel that persuading the protagonists to apologise and shake hands is sufficient, but that likewise is no guarantee that old wounds are healed. Making peace goes much deeper than that, and is far harder to achieve, for few situations are so straightforward that all it needs is to 'kiss and make up'. Ask those who have laboured over the years to bring peace to Northern Ireland, the Middle East, the Balkans and so forth, and I'm sure all would tell you that it is one of the most demanding tasks that anyone can be asked to undertake. Resolving any serious dispute involves the investment of time and energy, a significant element of personal risk, and a not inconsiderable degree of courage in tackling complicated and controversial issues into which one is inevitably drawn. In other words, peacemaking has nothing to do with offering pat answers or cosmetic solutions, papering over the cracks to secure peace at any price. It has nothing to do with keeping our heads down to avoid confrontation, and encouraging others to do the same. Rather, it entails a willingness to get alongside people and become involved in society in such a way that, just possibly, we can contribute to breaking down barriers, overcoming prejudice and dispelling mistrust, creating in their place bridges of acceptance, openness and solidarity that enable people to work together instead of pull apart. To be a peacemaker, then, far from being a somewhat naïve, well-meaning idealist, as some people imagine, means to get stuck in at the sharp end of life where people are hurting, in the hope of making a difference. To do that is truly to be a child of God, for it is to share fully in his reconciling purpose, his desire to draw all people to himself. Are we ready not just to look for peace, nor simply to long for it, but, above all, starting here and now in our daily relationships, to work to make it possible?

Pray

I wanted peace, Lord,
    an end to confrontation,
    so I bit my tongue,
    skirted the issue
    and hid my feelings.
Better that, I thought, than prolong the argument,
    allow a minor dispute to become a major row.
Yet life's not that simple,
    I realise that now,
    for the issue is still there,
    still rankling,
    still threatening to rear up and tear us apart.
It's not peace I've achieved,
    but a ceasefire,
    a temporary truce,

and unless we get things sorted,
thrash things out once and for all,
it's only a matter of time before swords are drawn once more
and hostilities renewed.
Lord,
save me from declaring peace where there is no peace,
from confusing running away with tackling the problem.
Give me the courage I need to face things head on,
sensitivity to stand in another person's shoes
and humility to listen, though I may not agree.
But teach me also,
openly and honestly,
to express my own point of view
and to engage in genuine dialogue,
speaking the truth in love.
Grant in all my dealings,
wherever relationships are broken and emotions raw,
that I might have sufficient love and concern,
patience and compassion,
to be a peacemaker –
an agent of your reconciliation,
in the name of Christ.
Amen.

Ponder

- Have there been times when, to keep the 'peace', you have run away from an issue rather than genuinely resolve it? Are you still doing that now?
- What things stop you from making peace in your own relationships, or helping to make peace in situations of confrontation and discord known to you?
- What would you say are the most important qualities needed to be a peacemaker? How far are these present in your life? What does this say about your discipleship?

Close

Gracious God,
    deliver me from all that separates me from you and others,
    and so help me in turn to break down barriers
    and to promote the harmony you desire for all people
    and all creation,
    through Jesus Christ,
    the Lord of all.
Amen.

Day 8: Blessing for those who are persecuted

Approach

Living God,
> teach me what it means to love and serve you,
> and, by your grace, help me to offer you wholehearted service,
> devoted discipleship
> and faithful witness,
> to the glory of your name.

Amen.

Read

Blessed are those who are persecuted for the sake of right; to them belongs the kingdom of heaven. Blessed are *you* when people abuse and harass you, making all manner of unfounded allegations against you because of me. Exult and celebrate, for you will be richly recompensed in heaven; in similar fashion they victimised the prophets before you.
Matthew 5:10-12

Reflect

Thankfully, some words of Scripture apply less today than to the time when they were first spoken, at least as far as you and I are concerned. I say 'thankfully' because such is the case with the words of Jesus concerning those persecuted for the sake of right. Such persecution might well bring a blessing, but it is at a price that most of us, myself included, would prefer not to pay. Indeed, should anyone relish the prospect of abuse, whether physical or psychological, we would consider there to be something seriously wrong with them. This final beatitude, then, is not, and never was, intended to encourage a desire for mortification, martyrdom or anything similar. Rather, it is intended to give hope, strength and encouragement to those facing testing on account of their faith, those for whom discipleship involves costly commitment.

The archetype of that, of course, was Jesus himself, who faced the emotional and physical trauma of Gethsemane and Calvary, not to mention hostility from many throughout his earthly ministry. For his early followers it was to be much the same story, several of the Apostles meeting a grisly end and Christians throughout the Roman Empire suffering all manner of hideous atrocities. For others again across the centuries, commitment to Christ has often involved harassment, torture and death; sometimes, grossly and paradoxically, at the hands of those who claimed to be Christians themselves, defending the true faith against heresy.

Was there a blessing for those who suffered in this way? Unquestionably there was, for as well as being promised the kingdom of heaven these also preserved the treasure of a clear conscience, the knowledge that they had stayed true to what they believed in to the very end. Most, I am sure, would have preferred to be spared such persecution, yet, for the joy set before them, and in the light of the joy they had already experienced in Christ, they were willing to endure whatever was asked of them.

Thankfully, as I've said, these words apply less to us today than to others across the years. We are free to worship, to believe what we will, to express ourselves, within reason, as we see fit. The worst hostility most of us are likely to suffer is small indeed. Occasionally, perhaps, we might be typecast and, in consequence, made the butt of people's jokes. We might possibly be treated as different, perhaps even resented if we dare to make a stand against wrongdoing or to hold out for what we see as non-negotiable Christian principles. In each case, though, that depends on whether we have the courage to declare our loyalties, to make plain where our allegiance lies. But here is the strangest of ironies, for though little is asked of us, compared with countless generations, we tend to give less, reluctant to risk even the outside chance of embarrassment, misunderstanding or mockery for the sake of the gospel. Rather than lose credibility or risk an adverse response, we keep our discipleship under wraps.

Is that true of us, even remotely? If so, what does it say about our faith, about our relationship with God in Christ? So little is asked of us for so great a reward. We want God's blessing, we talk blithely about it, but are we willing to pay the price – any price – to make it ours?

Pray

Lord,
    I'm not persecuted –
    not for my faith, my convictions or anything else –
    and for that I give you heartfelt thanks.
I'm free to worship you as I will,
    and to share my faith whenever and wherever I wish –
    a priceless heritage,
    hard-won by others –
    and I believe that you want me to celebrate that gift each day
    and safeguard it for generations to come.
For it's not a good thing, persecution –
    I can't believe you meant that –
    not something you'd ever want us to court
    or welcome for itself.
You want us, surely, to celebrate each day,
    to rejoice, without fear or reserve, not just in your love
    but also in the wonder and richness of life.
Yet don't let me hide behind that,
    avoiding any sacrifice,
    any possible hostility
    that faithful discipleship might entail.
If I need to make a stand,
    however unpopular,
    give me courage to make it.
If I need to say no to wrong,
    though it may cost me friends,
    give me integrity to do so.

If I need to speak of you,
    knowing others may ridicule or misinterpret,
    give me courage to continue nonetheless.
Whatever it might mean to be persecuted for righteousness,
    if you ask me to face that, give me grace to honour your call.
Teach me, then, to celebrate the freedom I have,
    but never to abuse it;
    to rejoice in the blessings of life,
    but, above all, to remember the blessings you promise to all
        who love you,
    and to live in such a way,
    however great the cost,
    as to make those mine.
Amen.

Ponder

- Has staying true to your faith ever cost you anything?
- Have you ever compromised your Christian convictions for fear of what the cost might be?
- In what ways today might Christian commitment involve 'persecution', false accusations, abuse or something similar?

Close

Sovereign God,
    give me strength to love you,
    serve you
    and stand firm for you,
    even when faith involves sacrifice
    and commitment entails cost.
Amen.

Day 9: Salt and light

Approach

Sovereign God,
  illumine my mind,
  blaze in my heart,
  sparkle in my spirit
  and shine through my life,
  so that others may glorify your name
  and rejoice in your goodness,
  through Jesus Christ my Lord.
Amen.

Read

You are the salt of the earth; but if salt is adulterated, how can its saltiness be restored? It no longer has any use, fit only to be thrown out and trampled underfoot. You are the light of the world. Just as a city situated on a mountaintop cannot be hidden, so nobody lights a lamp and places it under a bushel basket. They put it instead on a lamp-stand in order that it might shed light throughout the house. Similarly, let the light within you shine before others, so that they may see the good deeds you do and give glory to your heavenly Father.
Matthew 5:13-16

Reflect

Perhaps one of the most eloquent testimonies to how powerfully the words of Jesus have spoken to people across the centuries is the way some of them have become common coinage; idiomatic expressions that we use habitually without giving a second thought to where they first derived. Our verses today are a classic case in point. We talk, don't we, of those who contribute significantly to the good of others as being 'the salt of the earth', and when people fail to use latent gifts we speak of them 'hiding their light under a bushel'.

Would anyone, I wonder, use such expressions of us? If someone were to employ the first to describe us, we'd be delighted, flattered, proud, for we'd be making just the kind of impression that Jesus wants; no, not just *wants* but *expects*. But do we do that? Do we make any impression at all? Does anything about our way of life and discipleship make a sufficient difference to the lives of others for them to sit up and take notice, or for them to feel the poorer were it to be taken away? If not, then it's time for some serious soul-searching. You see, Jesus doesn't just say 'you could be the salt of the earth' or 'you could bring light to the world' but 'you *are* the salt of the earth' and 'you *are* the light of the world'. Why? Not because of any innate quality we possess but because of the gospel God has entrusted to us, and the way, through Christ and his Spirit, he has worked in our lives. To know and serve him is not to be perfect but it is in some way, however small, to reflect his light and give a taste of his goodness. If that is only through making known our faith, sharing a common kindness or reaching out to someone in need, we are, at least in part, fulfilling our calling.

There are, of course, many reasons why, generally speaking, we might hide our light under a bushel. We may be shy, unsure of ourselves, reluctant to push ourselves forward. We may be busy, feeling we do not have time to do a gift justice. We may be lazy, unwilling to make the effort to cultivate and use a talent. We might have other interests that take precedence, the gift in question low on our list of priorities. And so we could go on. In terms of ourselves that may not matter much, only we're talking here finally not about *us* but about *God*; about what *he* has given and what *he* asks, what he needs from you and me in order to fulfil his purpose. Hide *your* light, by all means, but don't hide *his*.

39

Pray

I wanted to shine, Lord,
    to live in such a way that people would see something different:
    a quality of love
    and generosity of spirit
    that would move them to give glory to you.
But I didn't.
The most I managed was a mere spark,
    the briefest flicker,
    kindled for a moment but then extinguished.
I wanted to be salt of the earth:
    to speak for you,
    live for you,
    love for you –
    testifying, through my care, concern and compassion,
    to your gracious purpose for all.
But, again, I didn't.
My thoughts were too much for self
    and too little for you,
    so that I scarcely made a difference to anyone
    or anything.
I want to bring you glory, Lord,
    but I can't do that through my own efforts
    or in my own strength,
    for there's nothing about me that's special,
    no qualities I possess to set me apart.
It needs *you* to shine through me,
    touching my heart and stirring my spirit in such a way
    that I yearn to reach out in your name.
It needs you to work within me,
    nurturing faith and inspiring commitment,
    so that my life might bear fruit for you.
It needs you to teach me,
    challenging me afresh each day with your word of life,
    and helping me to listen and understand
    so that I might testify to your saving grace.

In other words,
    instead of trying to shed light
    I need rather to draw closer to you
    so that I may reflect yours:
    a light that shines in the darkness,
    and that nothing shall ever overcome.
Lord,
    hear my prayer,
    and may the radiance of your presence fill me now,
    in the name of Christ.
Amen.

Ponder

- Is there any way that you can say your life reflects Christ? How much does it fail to reflect him?
- In what ways do you bring light to others?
- Is your faith predominantly about what God can do for you or what you can do for others?

Close

Living God,
    may the experience of your love,
    the reality of your grace
    and the knowledge of your constant presence
    continue to transform my life each day,
    so that I may live and work for you more faithfully
    to the glory of your name.
Amen.

Day 10: The letter and the spirit

Approach

Almighty God,
    may your word of old speak afresh today,
    bringing new vision,
    new faith
    and new commitment.
Speak now,
    and help me to listen,
    in the name of Christ.
Amen.

Read

Don't let anyone imagine I've come to do away with the law or the prophets. On the contrary, far from doing away with them I've come to fulfil them. I'm telling you straight, until heaven and earth are no more, not one detail of the law, not even a miniscule point of punctuation, will be discarded until the whole has been realised. Anyone, then, who flouts even the most incidental of these commandments, and encourages others to do likewise, will be reckoned the least in the kingdom of heaven. Mark my words, unless your faithfulness surpasses that of the scribes and Pharisees, you haven't a hope of entering that kingdom.
Matthew 5:17-20

Reflect

There was no denying it: according to the rules of the game, strictly understood, the player had to be sent off. He had earned a second booking, a second yellow card, and, in soccer parlance, two yellows make a red. Yet, despite the indisputable facts, the crowd rose as one to voice their protest. It hadn't been a violent foul, and the individual in question was not a dirty player.

Unquestionably he had been foolish, but everyone in the ground felt that the referee should have exercised a little discretion and gone by the spirit rather than the letter of the law.

It's not just in interpreting the rules of football that discretion is needed but in administering any set of laws, which, of course, is why a judge in a court case has considerable leeway when passing sentence. Two people may commit the same offence, yet one is sent to prison while the other is made to perform community service. It all depends on what factors are taken into consideration.

We need, I think, to keep all this in mind if we are to understand what Jesus meant when he talked of coming not to do away with the law and the prophets but to fulfil them. Surely we live under grace, not law, we might say. Doesn't Paul himself tell us that the requirements of the law were nailed to the cross, its yoke done away with once and for all? And yes, all that is true, but it is so for two reasons. First, because in Jesus the law's demands have been met and the promises of the Old Testament prophets fulfilled. Secondly, and equally important, the way of life that he proclaimed and exhibited encapsulates the spirit of the law in a way that the letter could never begin to. In his challenge to love our neighbour *and* our enemies, to turn the other cheek and go the extra mile, to forgive and refuse to pass judgement, to exhibit a pure heart and a poor spirit, he cut through the ritual and regulations laid down in the Pentateuch, everything coming down, as we shall see later, to the simple instruction, 'Do as you would be done by'. Here, as I understand it, is what he meant by having a faithfulness that surpasses that of the scribes and Pharisees. It involves living by the way of love, a way that offers no easy options, still less any abrogation of moral responsibility, but that sets all within the context of love, against which every decision must be based. No longer can we take rules off the peg and apply them rigidly come what may. No longer can we set down black and white prescriptions concerning the rights and wrongs of every action, each set for ever in stone. Instead of dogmatic judgements we have situation ethics; in place of the commandments declaring 'Thou shalt not' we have a new commandment,

'Love one another'. Have we understood that wonderful simplicity of the gospel? Have we moved on from narrow judgemental attitudes? Do we live not by the letter but by the spirit?

Pray

I saw the signs, Lord –
   'No parking',
   'No entry',
   'Keep off the grass',
   'Trespassers will be prosecuted' –
   and I realised, to my shame, that I see you like that:
   as someone who sets rules,
   regulations,
   boundaries on my behaviour,
   telling me 'Don't do this!'
   'Don't do that!' –
   setting out what's right and wrong,
   acceptable or unacceptable,
   all laid out in stark, uncompromising terms.
But that's not what I see in Christ –
   nothing like it!
I see in him the one who repeatedly pronounced forgiveness,
   who mixed with those condemned as sinners,
   and who challenged those without sin to cast the first stone;
   the one who emphasised not what we *can't* do
   but what we *can*,
   summing up the law in terms of a new commandment,
   the call to love.
Teach me, Lord, that this is no easy option
   or fudging of the issues,
   but, if taken seriously, a challenge far deeper,
   infinitely more costly and demanding,
   but expressing your will
   in a way that the letter of the law can never begin to.

Save me from a narrow, bigoted and self-righteous attitude,
    a preoccupation with rules and regulations,
    a hiding behind pious moralising
    that saves me from facing real issues,
    for real people,
    in real situations.
Teach me what it means to live by the law of love,
    and, by your grace, help me to do that as best I can,
    in every relationship,
    every action,
    every day,
    to the glory of your name.
Amen.

Ponder

- Do you see God as one who decrees what you should *not* do or who affirms what you *can* do?
- Do you think the Church today is guilty of being too strict morally or not strict enough? How would you sum up the spirit of the gospel rather than the letter?
- Do you find it easier to condemn the bad in people rather than affirm the good? How far does the latter sum up what it means to live by the law of love?

Close

Lord Jesus Christ,
    help me
    through honouring your commandment to love
    to honour all the commandments,
    testifying to the truth of the law and the prophets
    in word and deed,
    and giving daily expression to the fulfilment
    these have found in you.
Amen.

Day 11: Dealing with anger

Approach

Eternal God,
  slow to anger and swift to bless,
  teach me to know you better,
  to love you more deeply,
  and to serve you more ardently,
  so that something of you may be seen in me.
Amen.

Read

You will be aware that your distant ancestors were taught, 'Do not commit murder', and 'Anyone who commits murder will be held accountable'. But I'm telling you that you will be answerable to the council simply for being angry with a brother or sister, and if you call someone a fool you are asking to be consigned to the pit of fire. If, then, you are bringing a gift to the altar and, on reaching it, you remember that someone has something against you, leave your gift there before the altar and, before anything else, make your peace with that person; then come and offer your gift. If someone is taking you to court, make peace with the plaintiff as swiftly as you can, before you get there, or you may find yourself bound over to the judge, passed on to the warder, and consigned to prison. I tell you no lie, you'll be stuck there until you've reimbursed everything you owe.
Matthew 5:21-26

Reflect

Can you honestly say you've never felt angry? Of course not, and neither would you want to. Anger is a part of being human, and has a real place among the gamut of our emotions. Even Jesus was roused to an explosion of fury in the Jerusalem temple.

Confronted by evil, injustice and exploitation, anger is not only understandable but necessary. Yet that is the exception rather than the rule; the last thing we would want is to elevate anger in general to the status of a virtue. Properly harnessed, it can be channelled for good, but more commonly its effect is destructive, leading to consequences that both we and others regret. All too many have suffered cruelty and abuse – both mental and physical – as a result of uncontrolled temper, and there is no telling how many feuds and broken relationships have their origins in things said and done in the heat of the moment that have subsequently been allowed to fester. That is the reason, surely, why Jesus devotes such a significant part of his Sermon on the Mount to this theme. He knew all too well the devastating impact anger can have: the way it can lead us to words and actions we would never usually contemplate, and how it can escalate so swiftly into violence, hatred, bitterness and recrimination. Unless we are able to control it before it controls us, then we are like a child unwittingly toying with an unexploded bomb. Unless we are awake to its dangers, we may find a fit of rage setting in motion a chain reaction that it is almost impossible to keep in check.

Next time, then, you feel the red mist rising, stop and ask yourself what it's all about. Is your anger justified or is it more about your hurt pride, frustrated wishes or simple irritability? If the latter, then count to ten, consider the consequences and give yourself time to cool down. If the former, then pray for help to use that anger constructively, turning it to good rather than evil, to build up rather than destroy. Remember that ours is a God who is slow to anger and abounding in steadfast love, always ready to forgive and forget. If that is so of him, who are we to be any different?

Pray

Was I wrong to be angry, Lord?
I really don't know.
I thought at the time I was justified,
    my rage understandable,

47

and, if anything, more restrained than it might have been.
But now –
    with time to reflect,
    ponder,
    see things from the other side –
    I'm not so sure,
    wondering whether fury blinded me to reason,
    my response as much due to selfishness,
    wounded pride,
    bigotry,
    as any sense of justice.
But whatever the case,
    warranted or not,
    I was wrong in what followed:
    spitting out cruel, callous words,
    designed to wound,
    to vent my spleen,
    rather than resolve the argument.
And then, to fan the flames,
    raking over the coals day by day –
    that was unforgivable,
    for it was no longer fed by white-hot emotion
    but cold and calculated,
    petty vindictiveness rather than righteous indignation.
Forgive me, Lord,
    and help me to heal the wounds I've caused
    and the hurt I've given.
Teach me that anger has its place,
    but only as a tool for good,
    never a weapon for evil;
    and grant me wisdom to know the difference
    and to show it in all my dealings,
    through Jesus Christ my Lord.
Amen.

Ponder

- Are there things you have said and done in anger that you now regret? Is it time to swallow your pride, to admit you were wrong, and to say sorry?
- Do you grow angry over trivial things, yet fail to be moved to anger by the evils and injustices of this world? What does this say about your faith?
- Have you learned from times when anger got the better of you, or is it still able to control you?

Close

Loving God,
 teach me when it is right to be angry
 and when it is not.
When anger is justified,
 give me the words to say
 and wisdom to channel that anger into furthering your purpose;
 and when it is misplaced,
 help me to pause,
 to think again
 and to let go.
In Christ's name I pray.
Amen.

Day 12: Removing temptation

Approach

Sovereign God,
  guide, instruct, challenge and equip me,
  so that I may love and serve you better each day,
  and walk faithfully in your ways,
  strong in faith,
  secure in hope
  and resolute in purpose.
Amen.

Read

You will be aware of the teaching, 'You shall not commit adultery', but let me tell you this: any man who leers lustfully at a woman has already unconsciously committed adultery with her. If your right eye is your weak spot, pluck it out and throw it away; it is preferable for you to lose one part of your body than for the whole of it to be thrown into hell. And if your right hand is your weak spot, cut it off and throw it away; it is preferable for you to lose one part of your body than for the whole of it to go to hell.
Matthew 5:27-30

Reflect

'Now then, kids, cut that out!' If you haven't used words like those yourself, you'll nonetheless understand well enough what they mean. Most parents are willing to bend a bit on most issues, but there comes a point when enough's enough, when a certain course of action needs to be stopped before it gets out of hand. What seems innocent and innocuous now can all too easily develop a life of its own, leading to unwelcome and unforeseen consequences. It's precisely this danger, I believe, that Jesus had in mind when he spoke in graphic and seemingly shocking terms about cutting off our hand or gouging out our eye if it causes us to go astray. He wasn't advocating for a moment any kind of self-mutilation, but was employing the commonly used rabbinic teaching device of hyperbole; that is to say, deliberately overstating his case to drive his message home. The point he was making is not that we should cut *off* any part of our anatomy but that we should cut *out* anything that might prejudice our relationship with God, under-mining our discipleship. It's impossible to spell out exactly what such things might be because each of us has different weaknesses, different pressure points, different areas in our life where we are vulnerable. But *we* know deep inside the things that might cause us to stumble, the areas where temptation is strongest, the aspects of discipleship in which we find it hardest to stay true. We know the actions, places and people that are most likely to bring out the worst in us, stretching obedience and commitment to breaking point. Do we carry on regardless? Do we deliberately court trouble? Do we knowingly put ourselves in situations where we are likely to fall? 'Cut that out,' says Jesus, 'before it's too late. If you're serious about following me, do everything you can to make the path easy, to avoid putting obstacles in your way.' As Jesus will remind us later, the way that leads to destruction is wide and the way that leads to life narrow. There's no escaping that, but if through our own actions we make it narrower still, then we've only ourselves to blame.

Pray

I fell, Lord,
    let you down completely,
    and I'm sorry for that,
    ashamed of my weakness,
    the frailty of my commitment.
But I'm more sorry still that I set myself up to fall,
    knowingly putting myself in a situation
    where my weaknesses were exposed

51

and temptation was bound to strike,
almost impossible to resist.
I knew the dangers,
and should have steered clear,
but I was torn in two,
part of me yearning to do your will
but the greater part half-wishing to succumb
to the tempter's voice,
to indulge in forbidden fruit.
I suppose I thought it wouldn't matter,
that you'd overlook the occasional lapse,
forgive the odd transgression,
just as you've done so many times before.
And so you will,
no question,
your nature always to have mercy,
to pick us up and help us start again –
provided, that is, I still desire forgiveness,
still want to walk in your way.
But that's the crunch,
for if I give in today,
the chances are I'll give in tomorrow and the next day,
slowly losing sight of your will,
forgetting what it means to follow you,
drifting ever further from your side.
Forgive me, Lord,
and call me back before it's too late.
Give me strength not just to resist temptation
but also to avoid whatever might cause me to fall,
and so may I stay true to you
as you are invariably true to me,
through Jesus Christ my Lord.
Amen.

Ponder

- Are there areas in your life where you are particularly prone to temptation?
- Do you put yourself in situations where those areas are exposed?
- Do you need to face up to temptation and conquer it, or is the wiser course to do all you can to prevent it gaining a hold?

Close

Lord God,
   all good,
   all pure,
   all holy,
   forgive me the many ways I fail you
   and my own responsibility in that failure.
Teach me to shun temptation,
   avoiding as best I can whatever may cause me to stumble,
   and so may I walk, this day and always, in newness of life.
In Christ's name I ask it.
Amen.

Day 13: Respect for all

Approach

Sovereign God,
    help me to be faithful in all my dealings,
    whether with you or others –
    open in every relationship not just to others,
    but also to you within them,
    through Jesus Christ my Lord.
Amen.

Read

The teaching of old also has it that: 'Anyone who divorces his wife must give her a divorce certificate.' But I tell you rather that anyone who divorces his wife, except on the grounds of unfaithfulness, effectively leads her to commit adultery, and whoever marries such a divorced woman commits adultery in turn.
Matthew 5:31-32

Reflect

All but the most ostrich-like among us will be aware that divorce rates in this country are higher today than they have ever been, marriage held by many in scant regard. In terms of the break-down of family life, not to mention the hurt to so many hidden in that statistic, this is clearly cause for grave concern, but we should, I think, avoid being too simplistic in our response. Does God really want two people who are manifestly unhappy and unsuited to stay together for the rest of their lives? I find that hard to believe. Does he want a partner who is abused or bullied simply to take what's coming, enduring a lifetime of torment? Surely not. I would not want to undermine the institution of marriage for a moment, but sometimes the very act of getting married is a mistake, undertaken for the wrong reasons, to the wrong person

54

at the wrong time, and the resulting relationship becomes a travesty of what God intends married life to be. Why should he not offer to those in such a situation a second chance, just as he offers new beginnings in everything else?

Ah, but hang on, some might say: how about the words of Jesus in verses like those above? Doesn't this show that he was categorically opposed to divorce. It's a fair point, but with this passage at least we need to probe deeper to understand what Jesus was saying and why. In the society of his time, divorce was common and surprisingly easy to secure . . . or at least it was for a man. If a husband was unhappy with his wife, or simply tired of her, it was a relatively straightforward matter to put her aside and marry someone else. He could even indulge in extra-marital sex so long as the object of his desires was not married or betrothed to someone else, and in the early history of Israel it was seen as perfectly permissible for a man to have several wives, not to mention a string of concubines. For the woman, it was a different matter. She couldn't divorce her husband, full stop, for, according to the culture of her time, she was his property. As for sleeping with someone else, that was the ultimate crime, punishable by death. In other words, it was one law for men and another for women. A man could do more or less as he pleased, but a woman, cast off through no fault of her own, could find herself penniless, homeless, friendless and hopeless.

It was this flagrant injustice that motivated Jesus' words here. What's sauce for the goose, he effectively says, is sauce for the gander. There's no more reason why a man should be able to divorce a woman than she should be able to divorce him – and no less reason either. That's not to suggest Jesus approved of divorce – his words here suggest he didn't – but his concern, at least in this case, was to correct an anomaly in the law, not formulate a dogma; to emphasise that in God's eyes not only do women have the same rights and worth as men, but also each of us has equal worth, whoever we may be. Nobody, in other words, has the right to discriminate against people, abuse them or treat them as objects, whether on the basis of gender, colour, age, sexuality or anything else. That was a revolutionary idea then, and sadly it is still seen as such by some today, nowhere more so than in the Church. Though we talk of God's love for all, of the infinite value he places on each one of us, many still find themselves marginalised by their fellow Christians simply for who and what they are. Are we different? We may like to think so, but subtle and not-so-subtle prejudices can run much deeper than we may realise. The words of Jesus, apparently concerned merely with divorce, in fact issue a challenge to look carefully at our lives, and to ask whether the way we speak, act and relate to others shows as much respect for them as we would like to be shown to us.

Pray

Lord,
    I try not to be prejudiced,
    and, in terms of the major issues at least –
    issues like race and gender –
    I think most of the time I succeed.
Yet there's more to it than that, isn't there?
For, in a host of other ways,
    I still sum people up on the flimsiest of evidence,
    allowing vague assumptions to shape not just my perception
    but even sometimes my attitude and actions.
I observe the way people dress, look, speak and act,
    and look no further.
I get wind of their politics, convictions and beliefs,
    and bracket them accordingly.
Time and again, instead of reality, I deal in stereotypes,
    unable to see past the label to the person underneath.
Yet you see us as we are,
    each with our mix of good and bad,
    strengths and weaknesses,
    yet valuing every one of us as a unique individual,
    precious in your sight.
Forgive me, Lord, those times
    I have lost sight of people's distinctiveness,

their innate worth as human beings.
Forgive me when I have failed to give them
    the respect they deserve,
    pigeonholing rather than interacting,
    assessing according to conjecture and preconceptions
    instead of weighing up the facts.
Deliver me, Lord, from all the ways
    prejudice still poisons my relationships,
    so that I may recognise the true worth of all.
In Christ's name I ask it.
Amen.

Ponder

- Are you as unbiased as you think? Do certain prejudices still have a hold in your life?
- In what ways do intolerance and discrimination still scar modern-day society?
- Do you give those you deal with in your daily relationships the respect they deserve?

Close

Lord of all,
    teach me to see people for who they are,
    rather than allowing my attitude to be shaped
    by peripheral differences,
    such as race,
    gender,
    class
    or culture.
Help me to look behind the labels
    to the person you love and value –
    and, in consequence, to give all the respect they deserve.
Amen.

Day 14: Yes or no

Approach

God of truth,
    so live within me
    that all I say and am
    and think and do
    testifies to who you are
    and to your saving renewing grace,
    through Jesus Christ my Lord.
Amen.

Read

Once more, you will all have heard how your forebears of old were told, 'You shall not take empty oaths, but must fulfil whatever vows you have made to the Lord.' My advice, though, is not to make oaths at all, whether by heaven (for this is God's throne), by the earth (for this is his footstool) or by Jerusalem (for it is the city of the great King). Similarly, do not swear by your head, for you cannot change the colour of even one hair, whether white or black. Let 'Yes' or 'No' be sufficient when promising something; anything more than that originates from the evil one.
Matthew 5:33-37

Reflect

What's wrong with taking an oath? Of all the teaching in the Sermon on the Mount, this can seem the most puzzling. It is hard to see here the self-evident wisdom that characterises much else of what Jesus has to say. Yet once we dig deeper, the point of this injunction becomes surprisingly obvious and understandable. I don't think for a moment that Jesus is banning oaths *per se*. The swearing of an oath in court, for example, or to join a movement, club or organisation, would, I'm sure, pose no problem for him, provided at least there was nothing in the oath contrary to the spirit of the gospel. His concern, rather, was with the habitual use of oaths to reinforce statements, ostensibly vouching for their veracity. Apparently this was all too common in his time, many casually invoking the name of God, heaven or Jerusalem to lend weight to their words. Why are such oaths unnecessary, even undesirable? Quite simply, because if we're serious about following Jesus, then our integrity should never be in doubt, and it should be clear to all that we speak the truth and nothing but the truth. If that is so, then there is no need to reinforce what we say; our honesty is unmistakeable to all.

It makes sense, doesn't it? Suddenly what seemed a rather obscure injunction becomes a both profound and challenging message, for how many of us, I wonder, can claim such transparent truthfulness as a feature of our lives? I'm not suggesting that we're inveterate liars, but which of us hasn't at some time hidden behind half-truths, twisting or concealing facts to our own advantage? Which of us can be relied on to give a straight answer to every question, even if doing so might prejudice our prospects in some way or prove uncomfortable? Which of us will own up to a mistake, admit an indiscretion or confess a fault instead of struggling desperately to cover our tracks? It can be costly sometimes to tell the truth, and it requires wisdom and sensitivity to know when and how to speak it in love, but you will know as well as I that the person who can be trusted to do that is a special person indeed. Is that you? It could be . . . and it should be.

Pray

I didn't mean to lie, Lord.
It just happened,
    the words slipping out before I had time to think.
I was embarrassed, I suppose –
    ashamed of my foolishness and failure –
    so I simply shook my head and denied the charge.

Call it instinct, if you like,
    an automatic desire to save face,
    for let's be honest about *this* if nothing else:
    none of us likes to be caught out,
    shown up in public,
    and I'm no different to the rest.
But that's just the point, isn't it, Lord?
I *should* be different;
    not in any elitist sense –
    smug,
    sanctimonious,
    self-satisfied –
    but distinguished by an unpretentious honesty,
    a truthfulness patent to all.
I manage that sometimes,
    but less often than I'd like to think,
    on occasions taking refuge instead in half-truths or white lies,
    avoiding what I'd rather not face.
Yet all too easily one falsehood leads to another,
    each bigger than the first,
    until I find myself trapped,
    caught in a snare of my own making.
Forgive me, Lord,
    and grant me an upright heart and integrity of spirit.
Draw me closer to you,
    and fill me with the truth that will set me free,
    equipping me to live and work to your glory,
    through Jesus Christ my Lord.
Amen.

Ponder

- Is your honesty and integrity evident to all, or do you bend the truth to serve your own ends?
- What has caused you in the past to be less than truthful? What was the end result?
- Are there truths that you need to share, or would owning up to them now do more harm than good?

Close

Lord Jesus Christ,
    teach me not just to proclaim you as the way,
    the truth
    and the life,
    but to follow you faithfully,
    with total integrity,
    and with everything I am,
    so that my whole being speaks of you
    and for you,
    to the glory of your name.
Amen.

Day 15: That little bit extra

Approach

Living God,
 in Christ you have shown us a new way,
 an approach to life and to others different to that of the world.
Teach me what it means to follow that path,
 and help me to walk it faithfully,
 by the grace of Christ.
Amen.

Read

You will be aware of the saying, 'An eye for an eye and a tooth for a tooth.' My message to you, though, is very different. Do not resist an evildoer, but if someone strikes you on the right cheek, offer the other cheek too. If anyone decides to sue you and take your coat, let them have your cloak as well, and whoever forces you to go one mile, go with them a second also. Give to whoever begs, and do not turn away anyone wishing to borrow from you. You will have heard the words, 'Love your neighbour and loathe your enemy', but my advice to you is to love your enemies and pray for all who mistreat you, so that you may become children of your heavenly Father; for he makes the sun shine on the evil as well as the good, and the rain fall equally on the virtuous and the corrupt. Why should you expect a reward for loving those who love you? Tax-collectors do as much as that. Similarly, what's so special about welcoming simply your brothers and sisters? Don't the Gentiles do the same? No, be without fault, just as your heavenly Father is free from any flaw.
Matthew 5:38-48

Reflect

Many of you, no doubt, will make use of the UNICEF 'Jar of Grace' scheme each year, putting aside a set sum of money each mealtime as an expression of thanksgiving and a small gesture of solidarity with the world's poor. This year I urged both my children to put in a penny every time we ate together, but immediately my son protested. 'Not 1p,' he said. 'That's not enough! Ten pence more like.' 'It's a kind thought,' I told him, 'but 1p will be enough from you. We'll put in extra ourselves.' He thought for a moment, then shook his head. 'Maybe not 10p,' he said reluctantly, 'but I'm putting in 5p at least!' He was determined to do more than was asked of him. Youthful exuberance, perhaps? Childish enthusiasm betraying a lack of understanding of financial realities? Well, maybe, but there is a lesson nonetheless that we can all take away from his attitude. All too often when it comes to giving – whether it be to God in the form of Sunday offerings on to others in the form of donations to charity and other good causes – we tend to give as little as we can. If something is asked of us involving time and effort, it's the same story.

The way of Christ offers a complete contrast. It calls us not merely to give but to go on giving, to make time and yet more time, to put in effort and then further effort still; quite simply, it goes the extra mile. In the context of the Sermon on the Mount, that meant being ready, when asked to fulfil one's duty according to Roman law of carrying a soldier's burden one mile, to go beyond what was asked and carry it two. That's what's asked of us in turn – to gladly, freely and spontaneously do that little bit extra – and that, of course, is what Jesus meant by exceeding the righteousness of the scribes and Pharisees. For them, it was a question of doing what was *required* of them, of doing what they *must*; for us it is the privilege of doing what is *possible* for us, of doing what we *may*.

'Not 1p. That's not enough! 10p more like.' In terms of Christian giving that innocent response says it all, but what, I wonder, does it say of our giving today?

63

Pray

'Do I have to?' I thought.
'Can't they see I'm busy?'
Yes, I know it's a good cause,
    and of course I'd like to support it . . .
    in an ideal world,
    where time's no object,
    money no problem.
But it's not like that, is it!
There's the mortgage to pay,
    food to put on the table,
    children to get ready for school;
    there's the lawn to cut,
    washing and ironing to see to,
    jobs needing doing around the house –
    these and so much else,
    and I need two pairs of hands just to get those done,
    let alone anything more.
Make time for others?
Give to the needy?
I'd love to, truly,
    but there's only so much anyone can do,
    and it seems to me I'm doing it all already.
Is that how I argue, Lord?
I hope not,
    and I doubt I'd be quite so blunt,
    quite so grudging,
    yet, truth be told,
    beneath the good intentions,
    the pious veneer,
    that's the way my mind works sometimes –
    more often than I care to admit.
Instead of how much I can do, it's how little.
Instead of what I can offer, it's what I can keep back.
Instead of giving extra, it's cutting down on the fraction I
    occasionally give.

Forgive me, Lord,
> for I don't just impoverish others
> through such meanness of spirit,
> but also myself.

Teach me to follow Christ,
> who gave not just a proportion extra
> but everything.

May I learn from him that in letting go of self
> I gain hold of life abundant,
> that in giving I receive,
> and that in responding to others I respond above all to you.

In his name I ask it.
Amen.

Ponder

- How ready are you to put yourself out for someone else? How far is your faith just talk, and how far are you ready to put it into practice?
- How would you describe your giving of time, money and effort in the service of Christ: generous or sparing, spontaneous or grudging, sacrificial or selfish?
- In what ways can you go the extra mile in your dealings with others this week? Consider ways you can respond beyond what is asked or expected.

Close

Gracious God,
   you have shown us in Christ
   what it means to love not just a few
   but all –
   even those who hate and reject you,
   who throw love back in your face.
Inspire me by your Spirit
   and renew me in Christ,
   so that I may love others in turn,
   with the same depth and devotion,
   to the glory of your name.
Amen.

Day 16: Unassuming discipleship

Approach
Sovereign God,
>draw me close to you now
>and still closer each day,
>so that my love for you may be real,
>my devotion genuine,
>my service sincere
>and my commitment true,
>through Jesus Christ my Lord.
Amen.

Read
Think twice before making a public show of religious devotion aimed at impressing others; you will deny yourselves any reward from your heavenly Father. Whenever you make a donation to the needy, for example, don't blow your own trumpet as the hypocrites like to do – whether in the synagogue or out in the street – eager to milk the plaudits. Mark my words, they have received the only reward they are going to get. Instead, when you make charitable gifts, ensure that the one hand has no idea what the other is doing; what you give, in other words, known only to you; and your Father, who sees what is going on in the heart, will reward you . . . Similarly, whenever you fast, don't emulate the hypocrites by deliberately putting on a long face and pained expression to ensure that everyone knows all about your piety. I repeat, the only reward they can look forward to is the one they've already enjoyed. By contrast, when you fast, spruce yourselves up as you would for a feast, anoint your head with oil and wash your face, so that the only one who knows you are fasting is your Father, who knows your innermost thoughts and will reward you accordingly.
Matthew 6:1-4, 16-18

Reflect

Are you prone to making a big show of prayer or going to church, of almsgiving or fasting in public? Somehow, I doubt it. Such activities may have had street cred in the pietistic world of the scribes and Pharisees, but today they are more likely to elicit apathy than admiration, ridicule than respect. Not many nowadays are impressed by religious devotion, however zealous or committed it might be. So do the words of Jesus concerning parading our virtue no longer apply? In some ways, probably not, but though our world may be very different to that in which Jesus lived, our underlying humanity remains the same. We all like to show ourselves off in the best light, to be thought well of by others, and few of us can resist the temptation to make sure people are aware of our good deeds, even if it's only through the odd aside dropped casually into a conversation.

Is there anything wrong with that? Probably not, so long as we avoid it becoming the overriding motive for any service we offer, generosity show, compassion exhibit or kindnesses share. If that happens, then the deed is immediately devalued, for it becomes about us rather than others, another way of serving self rather than God. Furthermore, instead of being an expression of love, it becomes patronising and hollow, no longer sincere but a means to an end.

Don't parade your virtue, says Jesus, nor seek any kind of recognition for the good you might do. Don't give for what you can get out of it, but simply for the sheer joy of giving back to the God who has given you so much. Do that, and you will have discovered the secret of unassuming discipleship; what it means to follow the one who, 'though he was in the form of God, did not regard equality with God as something to be exploited but instead emptied himself, taking the form of a servant and sharing our humanity, and, having taken on human form, humbling himself to total obedience, even to the point of death – death on a cross' (Philippians 2:6-8).

Pray

Lord,
    I don't make a great show of prayer;
    quite the contrary –
    I far too rarely pray at all,
    days passing sometimes in which I forget you completely.
I don't trumpet my worship either,
    instead tending to conceal it from others,
    almost embarrassed, in some circles, to admit to faith
    or speak of commitment at all.
So there's no danger, in that sense anyway,
    of parading my piety on the street corner,
    of holding up my virtue for all to see.
Too often the problem's the opposite:
    my devotions so sporadic
    that people might miss them altogether,
    and my prayer life so weak that I couldn't crow about it
    even if I wanted to.
Yet I do sometimes preen myself in public, nonetheless,
    carefully ensuring,
    through a word here,
    a comment there,
    that any good I've done,
    any generous word or deed,
    is duly noted and applauded.
I want someone, somewhere, to say well done
    and to offer a pat on the back,
    a few words of praise –
    nothing fancy or over the top;
    just enough to show that my actions haven't passed unnoticed.
Forgive me, Lord,
    for even when I think I'm serving you I'm so often serving self,
    more eager to promote *my* name than bring honour to *yours*.
Teach me to give for the joy of giving,
    to love for the pleasure of loving

and to serve you for the privilege of serving,
letting that be reward enough.
Amen.

Ponder

- Are there ways in which you unconsciously parade your discipleship?
- Could it be that you come across as self-righteous to others?
- Do you sometimes make the converse mistake of being overly self-deprecating?

Close

Gracious God,
teach me to love and serve you without any pretentious show
or any sense of self-righteousness.
Whatever I may offer or sacrifice for your sake,
help me to do so joyfully,
spontaneously,
and without fuss,
rejoicing in the privilege of working for your kingdom
and seeking in everything to bring honour to your name.
Amen.

Day 17: A quiet retreat

Approach

Living God,
    meet with me here in the quietness,
    speak to me now as I make space
    away from the press of the world,
    hear and answer me as I bring my all before you –
    body, mind and spirit –
    and so may I walk with you always,
    every moment of every day.
Amen.

Read

When it comes to prayer, don't make the mistake that characterises the hypocrites. They like nothing more than to make a great show of praying, standing conspicuously in the synagogues or on street corners so that no one can miss them. The only reward they're going to get is the one they've obtained already. For your prayers, in contrast, go into your room, close the door and pray to your Father who sees into the inner recesses of your mind, and your Father, who sees in this way, will reward you.
Matthew 6:5-6

Reflect

'Go into your room, close the door and pray to your Father who sees into the inner recesses of your mind.' On the face of it, those words merely amplify what Jesus has already had to say about not parading our virtue in public, yet there is, I think, another lesson to be drawn from this passage, and it concerns the importance of setting aside time for quiet prayer and devotion; time, in other words, to reflect on and commune with God. Nowhere do we see

71

that better exemplified than in Jesus himself, in the way he repeatedly drew aside from the crowds and his disciples to make time and space for God. Those moments of contemplation and communion were his lifeblood, nurturing the bond he enjoyed with his Father, nourishing his spirit, and giving him the strength, faith and courage he needed to stay true to his calling. I've no doubt he made time also throughout his ministry for public worship, but he understood that a living relationship with God is essentially a personal matter, dependent on moments shared with him if it is to retain its freshness and immediacy.

How does that make you feel: encouraged or disheartened, reassured or troubled, inspired or depressed? The trouble is that most of us find personal devotion difficult, for a host of reasons. Partly, it's a question of time, so many other jobs, responsibilities and demands clamouring for our attention. Partly it's a question of language, many finding themselves at a loss for words in prayer or struggling to express their true feelings. Partly it's a question of credibility, some finding it hard to come to terms with apparently unanswered prayer or wrestling with doubts about how God might hear and respond. Partly, also, if we're honest, it's a question of commitment, prayer being very low on the list of our priorities compared with innumerable other things we'd rather be doing. The result is that personal devotion tends to go by the board.

So should we feel guilty about this? If we mean by that 'Should we worry that God might punish us for our failure to pray?' then the answer is a resounding 'No!' He may be disappointed at our forgetting him, grieved that we neglect to nurture our side of the relationship, but whatever the reasons for our failure his response is to reach out all the more, not to rebuke or chastise but to remind us afresh of his love. Far from eliciting guilt, then, these words of Jesus should give us fresh heart, for underlying them is the assurance that God is always there, waiting to meet with us if only we will respond. Fail to make time for such moments and we do indeed pay a price, for we lose our sense of God's presence and even lose touch with him altogether, but it is a price that we impose on ourselves, not one God demands from us. He is with you now, as he is with you always, as he is with us all. Make time in these few moments you have set aside, to get to know a little better the one who knows you inside out, and loves you just the same.

Pray

I wondered where you were, Lord,
  why you seemed so strangely absent,
  failing to hear my prayers,
  failing to respond.
It was as though faith was divorced from life,
  day after day lived with no reference to your will
  or any sense of your guidance and purpose.
But then the truth dawned:
  it wasn't *you* who was absent,
  but *me*.
You'd been there all along,
  waiting to meet me,
  to listen
  and to answer,
  present every moment of every day
  if only I would see it.
I'd rushed from one thing to another,
  scurrying here, there and everywhere
  in a bid to get things done,
  but I'd forgotten what mattered most:
  spending time,
  alone,
  with you.
I'd taken it for granted you'd be there,
  and I was right in that, at least,
  but I'd forgotten that, if I want to hear your voice
  and feel your closeness,
  I need to be there too,
  listening,

73

learning,
giving
and receiving,
getting to know you as you know me.
Teach me, Lord, next time you seem distant,
next time I wonder why you've lost touch,
to pause
and ponder,
and to remember that, in all likelihood,
you're asking the same question of me,
only in your case,
unlike mine,
with good cause!
Amen.

Ponder

- Do you regularly make time for God in your daily routine?
- What things prevent you from spending time with God? What can you do to overcome these?
- What do you find most helpful in breathing life into your personal devotions? Are such devotions as meaningful as they used to be? Are there aids to devotion that might be worth exploring?

Close

Gracious God,
whatever else I may forget,
teach me to remember you
and to make time for you each day,
so that I might know you,
love you
and serve you better,
to the glory of your name.
Amen.

Day 18: Simple prayer

Approach

Sovereign God,
   mighty and mysterious,
   great and wonderful,
   I thank you that though you defy human expression
   I can speak to you one to one,
   knowing that you hear and respond.
In that assurance, I come now,
   seeking to hear your word
   and understand your will.
Amen.

Read

When praying, do not pile up empty words in the way the Gentiles do, imagining they will be heard because of their eloquence. Do not copy them, for your Father knows everything you need before you even ask him.
Matthew 6:7-8

Reflect

Few things are more annoying, are they, than people who never stop to listen? You know the sort: those who suffer from verbal diarrhoea, never letting you get a word in edgeways. There you are, desperate to chip into the conversation, to add your two penny-worth, only to be subjected to a seemingly endless monologue.

I wonder if God ever feels that way about us, for, if your prayers are anything like mine, he too must often feel bombarded by a barrage of words. We don't do it consciously; it just ends up happening that way. Not only is it generally us doing all the talking in prayer, but the talking tends also to be all about *us*. We may begin with a few token words of praise and thanksgiving, but the 'meat' of our prayers tends to be what concerns us personally: our needs, desires, troubles and anxieties; our families and friends; our hopes and aspirations; the routine business of our daily lives – perhaps with a smattering of intercession thrown in for good measure. There's nothing inherently wrong with any of that, of course, except that it's hopelessly one-sided, just one aspect of what God intends prayer to be.

Compare such prayers with the model Jesus sets out in the so-called Lord's Prayer, Matthew 6:9-13, for the content could hardly be more different. What do you notice most about that model? To me, one thing stands out: the prayer is more about God than us, more about his will than our desires, more about his kingdom than our lives! It begins by acknowledging his greatness and moves on to seek his will, only then turning to us – and even at this point the focus is on the bare essentials of life, the need for forgiveness, and a request for help to stay true to God's way in times of testing. In other words, the prayer is God-centred rather than self-centred.

Surely this is what Jesus had in mind when he advocated simple rather than long-winded prayers. To treat prayer as a shopping list is to misunderstand what it's all about, overlooking the importance of focusing on God, of recognising his greatness and seeking a greater understanding of his purpose both for our lives and for the world in general. It's about aligning ourselves with God rather than expecting him to align himself with us, about yearning to grow in grace so that we might be more effective in his service – all of which can only happen if, as we explored in the last session, we spend time quietly and reflectively in his presence, listening for his voice rather than indulging our own. Does that sound hard? It's not meant to, for God understands the impulse to pour out our concerns, worries and hopes, and I've no doubt he responds wherever and whenever he can, but though such prayer may yield its rewards it will not give us that closeness to God that is prayer's ultimate purpose. Next time you pray, then, spend a little less time talking and a little more listening. You won't be disappointed.

Pray

Was it a prayer, Lord?
It was meant to be,
    and of course it was, to a point,
    yet I came away feeling frustrated,
    unsatisfied,
    as though something was missing,
    as though I hadn't got through.
I see it now,
    your word suddenly clear:
    I spoke *to* you, not *with* you,
    scarcely pausing for breath to listen;
    more intent on listing *my* wishes than seeking *your* will,
    with having *my* say than hearing *your* word.
You listened, no doubt –
    graciously and lovingly as ever –
    but you knew what I needed before I asked you,
    and you knew, too, that my greatest need
    was simply to spend time with you –
    quietly,
    reflectively,
    reverently –
    focusing on your goodness,
    recognising your love
    and rejoicing in your grace.
Teach me to do that, Lord:
    to understand that prayer is more than a wish list,
    a catalogue of requests.
May it be instead an encounter,
    a time of meeting,
    an opportunity to glimpse your purpose
    and to commit myself more fully to it,
    giving you always, in all things,
    the praise, glory, honour and worship that is due to you,
    this day and for evermore.
Amen.

Ponder

- How much are your prayers about you and how much about God?
- Do you make time for silence in prayer as well as words? Do you find words a help or a hindrance?
- In what ways, if any, do you expect and allow God to answer your prayers?

Close

Sovereign God,
    when I come to you in prayer,
    instead of bombarding you with words,
    besieging you with requests
    or assaulting you with demands,
    teach me simply to draw near
    and to spend time in your presence
    in quiet communion and companionship.
So may I hear your voice,
    discover your will,
    and receive your guidance,
    through Jesus Christ my Lord.
Amen.

Day 19: Our Father

Approach

Gracious God,
>alongside your holiness teach me to recognise your love,
>alongside your power to glimpse your tenderness,
>alongside your justice to understand your grace.

Reveal to me each day more of your mercy, compassion,
>gentleness and care,
>and may that knowledge sustain and inspire me,
>now and always.

Amen.

Read

Instead, when you pray, use words like these: Our Father in heaven . . .
Matthew 6:9a

Reflect

It's often said that we can fail to see what's right under our very noses, and if ever that was true it must surely be with the Lord's Prayer. It's so familiar to most of us that, try as we might, we find it well-nigh impossible not to repeat it parrot-fashion so that we fail to appreciate its depths or to understand the wonder of what we're saying. That wonder begins with the very first two words: Our Father. We're so used to thinking of God in such terms that we scarcely give it another thought, but for the disciples, hearing Jesus use this form of address for the first time, it was revolutionary stuff: at once shocking and sensational, frightening and thrilling. Can any of us truly presume to approach God with such familiarity – the same God who, according to the Old Testament, no one can look upon and live; the God who, hitherto, could only be approached in the holy of holies via the mediation of the high priest; a God enthroned over all: holy, righteous, sovereign? Is it possible to enter into a personal 'family' relationship with him rather than one based on awe, penitence, even fear? It must have seemed too good to be true, yet this is precisely the kind of relationship Jesus wanted not just for them but for us; a relationship that he goes on making possible day by day.

Is that how we perceive God? Is that how we approach him? Is that how we understand prayer? We may think so, but before we answer too readily, it might pay to stop and reflect for a moment on parent/child relationships. If things are as they should be, then this should be marked by particular qualities: love, trust, respect, commitment, care, affection, and so on. As Jesus says later in this sermon: 'Ask, and you will receive; search, and you will find what you're looking for; knock, and the door will be thrown open. For whoever asks receives, and whoever searches finds, and to whoever knocks, the door will be opened. Would any among you, should your child ask for bread, give a stone? Or if asked for a fish, would you give a snake? If then, you who are flawed, know how to give good gifts to your children, how much more will your heavenly Father give good things to those who ask him!' (Matthew 7:7-11)

Children, ideally, should be able to approach their parents in the knowledge that their very presence brings delight; that responding to their needs is a pleasure, not a chore; that their welfare, peace of mind, security and happiness are always of paramount importance. That, says Jesus, is how God feels about us, and that is the confidence in which he wants and expects us always to approach God in turn.

All this is not to say, of course, that he will grant every request, come what may; as every parent knows, that would be hopelessly to spoil a child. Nor is it to say that he *can* guarantee happiness; there are limiting factors within this world of ours that God, in his wisdom, has chosen to bind himself by. What it is to say is that nothing ultimately will induce him to give us up, any more than, in normal circumstances, loving parents would happily give up a child of their own. The conviction at the heart of our faith, under-pinning each moment of every day, is that we are not part of an impersonal meaningless universe but infinitely valued as children by one who calls himself, simply yet wonderfully, 'our Father'.

Pray

Lord,
    I need a sense of your strength:
    your sovereign power,
    able to move mountains and change lives,
    fashioning the very universe we inhabit,
    constantly at work to fulfil your purpose –
    the beginning and end of all.
I need a sense of your holiness:
    your passion for all that is good and true,
    pure and lovely,
    and your sorrow over everything that demeans your creation
    and frustrates your purpose,
    separating person from person
    and all from you.
I need a sense of your otherness:
    your utter transcendence
    before which I can only kneel in reverence and wonder,
    homage and humility,
    offering my heartfelt praise and worship,
    for you are beyond words,
    beyond comparison,
    defying definition.
I need all that, Lord,
    and I thank you for it,
    but I need also, and especially, to recognise you as a God of
        love:
    the one who nurtures me like a little child;
    who cherishes,
    strengthens,

comforts,
teaches,
heals,
helps
and holds –
quite simply, my Father.
Amen.

Ponder

- What picture do you have of God? What aspect of God does this most emphasise?
- In what ways do you think of God as 'Father'?
- Does a parent/child relationship sum up the way you approach God in prayer?

Close

Living God,
I praise you that though you are above all,
beyond all,
before all
and over all,
you invite me to call you 'Father';
the relationship you want me to share with you
being one of love rather than fear,
friendship rather than slavery,
closeness rather than detachment.
For the warmth of your welcome,
the breadth of your goodness,
the richness of your grace
and the wonder of your care,
Father, I thank you!
Amen.

Day 20: Hallowed be your name

Approach

Sovereign God,
   I come to you in prayer,
   seeking to offer my worship
   and to bring my praise.
I come to acknowledge your greatness
   and to declare your steadfast love.
Accept what I offer,
   and teach me to honour you in all I am and do,
   to the glory of your name.
Amen.

Read

. . . hallowed be your name.
Matthew 6:9 (NRSV)

Reflect

'Hallowed be your name' – it's a curious expression, isn't it? When did you last hallow anything? Yet we use those words time and again as we repeat the Lord's Prayer. So what do we mean by them? What, if anything, do we think we're saying when we employ this somewhat archaic phrase? To understand that, it might help to think in terms of honouring someone who has died, or perhaps living up to our family name. In the first case, the greatest tribute we can possibly pay is not erecting some plaque or memorial but carrying on the deceased person's work, building upon it, helping to further the things which that individual held dear. In the second case, our aim will be to bring credit upon our family, to reflect well upon them, to keep a tradition alive. Perhaps an even better analogy might be the way a multinational company takes care to safeguard the standing of its brand name. No effort is spared to ensure that this name is held in esteem, trusted, associated with all that is best in terms of quality, reliability and service. To hallow, in other words, means to bring glory and honour, admiration and regard.

So it is with the Lord's Prayer, only this time the name in question is God's. When we say 'hallowed be your name' we are not simply asking that everyone may know about God or that his name will be safeguarded from blasphemy. Our prayer, rather, is that everything he stands for may be acknowledged, valued, held high, so that people everywhere might recognise the sort of God he is and the sort of world he yearns for. And that, of course, begins with us. If we who profess his name don't honour him, why should anyone else? If our lives don't testify to his transforming power, why should anyone take notice of the claims of the gospel? If the things we practise do not accord with the things we preach, why should anyone take our message seriously? To pray the Lord's Prayer means, at the very start, to commit ourselves to doing all in our power to honour God's name, striving as far as is humanly possible to make our words and deeds one.

'Hallowed be your name'; it's a curious phrase, undoubtedly, but a powerful one, more powerful than we might have realised – easy to say, but hard to live up to.

Pray

I've said it so many times, Lord –
    'hallowed be your name' –
    without ever thinking what it means.
I repeat it routinely,
    almost out of habit,
    imagining that the fulfilment of those words is down to you
    rather than me.
I'm right, in part, of course,
    for bringing you honour doesn't just rest on my shoulders –
    pity help you if it did!
But if I don't mean business when I pray those words,
    then I've no right to pray them,

for I stand condemned by my own mouth,
    exposed by my false piety.
Do I honour you? – that's the question.
Does anything in my life proclaim your kingdom,
    reflect your love,
    redound to your glory?
I hope so, Lord,
    and I pray so,
    but I know that whatever does,
    far more doesn't.
So today my prayer is short and simple:
    help me not just to ask that your name be honoured,
    but, above all, to honour that prayer.
Amen.

Ponder

- Do the things you say and do reinforce the worship you offer to God? In other words, do you practise what you preach?
- What do you think it means to honour God? How far do you attempt to do that?
- Are there aspects of your life that dishonour God's name?

Close

Loving God,
    teach me that asking for your name to be honoured
    is not enough:
    that as well as words I must offer deeds –
    a life that brings you glory
    and that honours everything you stand for,
    all you represent.
So, then, work within me
    until all I am, think, say and do promotes your kingdom
    and redounds to your honour,
    through Jesus Christ my Lord.
Amen.

Day 21: On earth, as it is in heaven

Approach

Living God,
 equip me through your word,
 inspire me through your Spirit
 and renew me by your grace,
 that I may share in the work of Christ
 and the growth of your kingdom.
In his name I pray.
Amen.

Read

May your kingdom come and your will be done on earth, as it is in heaven.
Matthew 6:10

Reflect

At the last General Election in the UK a disturbing trend became all too apparent: people across the country, and especially young people, are losing interest in politics. Does that matter? I think it does, for a variety of reasons. It suggests first that people are disillusioned with politicians, no longer trusting them as they once did; most people, in fact, barely believing what they say at all. Rightly or wrongly, Westminster in particular has become associated with spin and broken promises, with many words disguising little action. If that's a problem in itself, perhaps a greater one is that fewer and fewer people appear to believe in the political process, and thus ever-fewer are becoming involved in the decision-making forums of society. Perhaps most troubling of all is the implication that people have given up believing things can change, resigning themselves instead to making the best of a bad job.

As Christians, similar cynicism can strike at the very heart of our faith. We talk of the kingdom of God, and we repeat the words of the Lord's Prayer, 'Your kingdom come', but we conveniently forget the line that follows this, 'on earth, as it is in heaven'. Can that ever begin to happen, we ask ourselves? One look at the ills that beset our world would seem to suggest otherwise. Some perhaps have occasionally dared to dream – at the end of a world war perhaps, at the inception of the welfare state, at the end of the Cold War, and so on – but for each evil ended another has begun, and for every new dawn there seems a corresponding twilight. Is there any prospect of witnessing God's kingdom here on earth? It would be an idealist indeed who expects to see such in his or her lifetime, but that should not stop us from trying to bring it closer. And that takes us back to what I was saying earlier about politics. People may have lost faith in the established channels of debate but not all have given up believing things can change. Many have resorted to what is termed 'direct action', whether that means a march of protest, a peace camp or an anti-roads sit-in. We may applaud such efforts or condemn them, depending on our point of view and the methods employed, but no one can deny the commitment many show to their cause, or question the firmness of their convictions.

As followers of Christ we are called to direct action of a different sort. Every deed of love, act of service, extension of forgiveness, gesture of compassion or expression of faith contributes to the fulfilment of God's purpose, the promotion of his kingdom here on earth. These may not seem much and their impact may appear small, but they are a beginning; as the old proverb has it, 'drop by drop fills the bucket'. One thing is certain, if we want to see change, we have to help make it happen. To pray 'Your kingdom come' is not simply to express pious hopes about the distant future but to commit ourselves to the present. It means, instead of asking when that kingdom may come, asking rather what we personally are doing to help bring it nearer.

Pray

I lose faith sometimes, Lord,
    I don't mind admitting it.
When I look around me,
    and see the mess I make of my life,
    the mess we make of the Church
    and the mess we make of our world,
    I can't help feeling sometimes that it's hopeless,
    any suggestion that things might change for the better
    simply pie in the sky,
    cloud-cuckoo land.
For all my good intentions and bold resolutions,
    I'm still much the same person I've always been.
For all the rhetoric of politicians,
    musings of philosophers,
    efforts of activists
    and advances of science,
    the world seems no better than in years gone by;
    if anything, slightly worse.
What reason to think things can be different?
What grounds do I have for hope?
Only then I come back to you –
    to your power shown on the cross:
    renewing and redeeming,
    bringing hope out of despair,
    joy out of sorrow,
    and life out of death –
    power that has changed lives across the centuries
    and that goes on changing them today.
I still lose faith sometimes –
    I can't help it,
    for I inevitably look at life with my eyes rather than yours,
    but when I start to do that, Lord,
    remind me again of who you are
    and what you've done.
Remind me that you are greater than the mind can conceive,

sovereign over all,
mighty beyond words –
and so may I trust in your power,
working within me and all,
able to accomplish more than I can ever ask or begin to imagine,
to the glory of your name.
Amen.

Ponder

- Do you see the kingdom of God as something that will come in the distant future or as already having begun here on earth?
- What are you doing to help make that kingdom more real?
- Do you still have a sense of what God is able to do in human lives and the world today?

Close

Sovereign God,
    instead of promoting my purposes
    may I seek yours;
    instead of furthering my own ends
    may I pursue your interests;
    instead of striving to achieve my goals
    may I labour first to build your kingdom.
Teach me what it means to pray 'Your will be done',
    and help me not just to *say* those words
    but also to *mean* them.
Amen.

Day 22: Daily bread

Approach

Loving God,
  teach me to celebrate all you have provided
  and to share it,
  rather than to hanker for ever more,
  and to hoard it.
Amen.

Read

Give us each day our daily bread.
Matthew 6:11

Reflect

'And this,' said the couple, showing me round their delightful and luxurious cottage, 'was another answer to prayer. We asked God to provide the right place and this is what he's given.' They were evidently sincere, and there was no way anyone could fault their commitment, yet I couldn't help but question whether prayer had anything whatsoever to do with their plush new home. Does God really provide us with the perks of life, whether that is a new home, good job, decent income or so forth? If so, it's hard not to ask why he allows others to face homelessness, hunger, poverty and all manner of other privations. It sits even less easily with the repeated teaching of Jesus in the Gospels concerning renouncing material blessings, and it sits least comfortably of all with the words of the Lord's Prayer: 'Give us each day our daily bread.' The meaning here is straightforward enough: not 'give us a sumptuous feast, a slap-up meal'; not even 'give us a good feed'; but give us enough of what we *need*. There is admittedly a strand of teaching in the Old Testament that equates prosperity with God's blessing, labelled the Deuteronomic history by biblical theologians, but this was forcibly countered by other Old Testament writers, not least in the book of Job.

All this is not to say we shouldn't be thankful for the blessings life puts our way, whether through our own efforts, good fortune or accident of birth. Everything ultimately belongs to God, and a proper sense of gratitude will spill over into a responsible and generous stewarding of what he has given, but we should, I think, be cautious in postulating a direct link between material blessing and answered prayer; and even more cautious about ever praying for material things. The model Jesus gives is, as we have seen, altogether different: 'Give us each day our daily bread.' In other words, give us what we need to get by; not what we would like but what we can't do without. It is a request that fits in with everything Jesus has said about treasures on earth and in heaven, about serving God and money, about seeking above all else the kingdom of God and his righteousness. This single line comprises the sole instance within the Lord's Prayer of asking God to provide for our personal needs. The only other similar requests are for forgiveness, protection from temptation and deliverance from evil, but each of these is concerned simply with faithful discipleship rather than personal gain.

How do your prayers compare to this? How much are they concerned with God providing for your wishes and how much with *you* fulfilling *his* will? Faith is not a celestial investment scheme, guaranteeing lucrative dividends in the here and now. It does not offer access to some heavenly slot machine, promising a bumper payout if we put in sufficient prayer and supplication and come up with the right devotional combination. It is rather the conviction that, whatever we face, God will sufficiently meet our needs – physical, emotional and spiritual – for us to stay true to him and to persevere in his service until our journey's end. Then, and only then, are we guaranteed his unreserved, unlimited and unending blessing.

Pray

I prayed, Lord . . .
   I waited . . .
   and nothing happened . . .
   my request not granted,
   my faith, it seemed, in vain.
And I was puzzled,
   disappointed,
   even angry,
   wondering why you'd let me down,
   why my faithfulness in prayer
   and diligence in devotion
   had apparently been spurned –
   unanswered and unrewarded.
And then I read those words again –
   'Give us each day our daily bread' –
   and I realised it wasn't you at fault
   but me,
   for I'd failed to listen or learn,
   my prayer more about desires than needs,
   about life's little extras
   rather than the things that really matter.
It wasn't daily bread I was asking for,
   but daily treats –
   health, wealth and such like,
   whether for me or my loved ones –
   and of course there's nothing wrong with those;
   quite the contrary:
   you delight to see all creation rejoicing in your blessings,
   celebrating your countless gifts.
Yet, above all, you want me to experience
   the sheer joy of knowing you,
   the wonder of understanding more fully
   the extent of your love
   and the breadth of your purpose.
Teach me, then, not to dwell on myself in prayer,

or on my own small world,
but to focus on you,
recognising who you are,
what you have done
and what you have yet to do.
Help me to open my life to your living word
and your transforming grace,
so that I may receive not merely daily bread
but also food for my soul,
nourishment that satisfies now and always.
Amen.

Ponder

- How big a part does the acquisition of possessions play in your life?
- What do you expect God to provide for you: daily bread or something more?
- How much are your prayers concerned with physical desires and how much with spiritual needs?

Close

Faithful God,
teach me to be content with what I *have*
rather than to bemoan what I *wish* I had;
to focus on what I *need*
rather than dwell on what I *want*;
to appreciate the *essentials* of life
rather than constantly to crave its *luxuries*.
Help me, in other words,
to celebrate the things that matter,
and to let go of those that don't.
In Christ's name I pray.
Amen.

Day 23: The key to forgiveness

Approach

Merciful God,
    unworthy though I am, I come to you
    seeking your redeeming, renewing and restoring touch.
Meet with me in your word
    and through your Spirit,
    so that I may rejoice afresh in your love
    and show it in my dealings with others,
    to the glory of your name.
Amen.

Read

. . . and forgive our mistakes as we forgive those who wrong us. If you forgive others their mistakes, your heavenly Father will forgive you in turn; but if you refuse to forgive them your Father will withhold forgiveness from you in turn.
Matthew 6:12, 14-15

Reflect

To understand what forgiveness means in terms of our relationship with God, I want you to picture yourself in a somewhat sticky situation. Imagine that you've lost concentration while driving and have been pulled over by the police for speeding. You weren't just a little over the speed limit but way beyond it, so that you have no reason whatsoever to expect any clemency, despite your evident shame and profuse apologies. Perhaps if your licence was clean you might just possibly hope for a stern telling-off and nothing more, but no, you've been guilty of the same offence and numerous others countless times before. Little wonder, then, that you fear the worst. But what's this? Impossible surely!

Without even wanting to see any documentation the policeman is sending you on your way, with just a cautionary word. Amazing!

Whether it would be good for police to show such leniency is questionable to say the least, but that is the sort of forgiveness God shows us. Though we repeatedly transgress against him, stepping hopelessly outside his commandments, he is always willing to give us another chance. Though we fail him time and again, if we acknowledge our mistakes and genuinely seek forgiveness, then as far as he's concerned there is no record of them; it's as though they've never been.

So that's it, then? We just need to express sorrow to receive forgiveness? Well yes . . . and no. It all depends on what we mean by being sorry, for, as we saw earlier, in relation to God such sorrow needs to be active as well as passive. True remorse shows itself in a desire to change, to show that our expression of regret is more than simply empty words; and, according to Jesus, the best way to do that – perhaps, even, the only way – is to forgive others in turn.

Is God's forgiveness conditional then on our forgiving others? It can't be, for if it was we'd all be in a sorry pass. Moreover, it would make God's love dependent on works rather than faith. Yet, if nothing else, we must surely *aim* to forgive, even if we fail. If the intention to do so isn't there, then we deny ourselves God's forgiveness, not because he withholds it but because we haven't grasped what it means and so are unable to make it ours. Next time, then, you come before God, seeking his mercy, begging for pardon, stop and ask yourself whether others are asking the same of you, and whether you've really understood what forgiveness is all about.

Pray

I meant to forgive, Lord,
    to put the past behind me and start afresh,
    and I honestly thought I had –
    apologies accepted and all that stuff.

But I see now that I was wrong,
    for I've raked things up again;
    mistakes long past,
    which we both thought were dead and buried,
    plucked from the ashes,
    rekindled,
    and hurled in white-hot accusation.
It was a shock, Lord,
    for I truly believed I'd dealt with the matter,
    any last flickering flame of anger finally extinguished,
    but somewhere, deep within, the embers were still smouldering,
    needing only a few fresh coals to reignite the fire.
It's more complicated than I imagined,
    this business of offering real, unreserved pardon,
    for hurt is hard to quench,
    bitterness difficult to douse,
    but I need to smother the blaze once and for all,
    for it's consuming my relationships,
    not just with others
    but, worst of all, with you.
Lord,
    have mercy.
Teach me to forgive as you have so faithfully forgiven,
    to show the same gracious and generous pardon
    that you so freely offer all.
Remind me afresh of your overflowing love
    and unfailing grace,
    and may that shape all I do and am,
    to your praise and glory.
Amen.

Ponder

- Have you received the forgiveness God longs to show you?
- Are there those you find it impossible to forgive? Does the bitterness you feel prevent you from fully accepting God's forgiveness?
- How far is forgiving others conditional on them being sorry and seeking pardon?

Close

Gracious God,
    remind me afresh each day
    of your love that goes on reaching out,
    your mercy that know no bounds,
    your patience that is never exhausted
    and your goodness that nothing can exhaust,
    and so may I live each day in constant celebration,
    responding to your great faithfulness in joyful service.
Amen.

Day 24: Rescue us from evil

Approach

Living God,
> teach me afresh today that, whatever life may bring
> and whatever I might face,
> nothing finally will ever be able to separate me from your love
> or your eternal purpose in Jesus Christ my Lord.

Amen.

Read

Save us from falling prey to temptation, and rescue us from evil.
Matthew 6:13

Reflect

'Rescue us from evil' – we'd all say Amen to that, wouldn't we? But what are we actually asking for? Can prayer ever inoculate us against suffering and sorrow, heartache and hardship? The answer, of course, is no. Tragedy afflicts the Christian as much as anyone else. Pain is just as real, illness just as likely, ultimately death as inevitable for us as it is for the next person. If we suppose saying a prayer each day is going to protect us from such things we are sadly deluded. God, I am sure, does not wish them upon us for a moment, but they are part of life as we know it, an inescapable facet of being human. So why does Jesus teach us to pray, 'rescue us from evil'? To understand that we need to recognise first that the evil he has in mind is something altogether different, referring instead to anything and everything that might separate us from God. These may come in various guises: in the temptation flagrantly to turn our back on God and flout his will; in more subtle pressures to compromise and dilute our faith, unwittingly denying it through an imperceptible but inexorable blurring of the edges; in circumstances and events that apparently contradict belief, causing us to question our faith or lose it completely. These pressures and temptations are stronger and more common than we might imagine, and, however committed we might think ourselves to be, none of us, through our own efforts, can be confident of not falling. We need God's strength and support; his Spirit within to guide and counsel, equip and inspire; his grace to lift us up when we stumble and encourage us forward once again.

We cannot claim any special exemption from the challenges life might dish out, but we can claim God's help in meeting them, the assurance of his presence by our side through the darkest valley and deepest shadows. *He* will not let go of us but *we* can all too easily let go of him. That is why we pray 'rescue us from evil' – both to remind us of the threat we're up against and to seek God's help in meeting it.

Pray

'Lord, save me!' I cried.
'Protect me!'
'Deliver me!'
But disaster struck nonetheless,
    bringing heartbreak,
    hurt,
    confusion.
'Lord, bring healing!' we begged.
'Bring wholeness!
'Make well!'
But there was no happy ending,
    no sudden and miraculous recovery –
    just the harrowing and lingering death of one we loved.
And I threw up my hands in anger,
    asking 'Why?'
'How?'
'Where was God when we needed him?'

99

It shook me to the core,
    my faith buckling,
    all but broken,
    until I remembered that those words, 'rescue us from evil',
    were spoken by your Son
    who went on to face evil at its fiercest,
    suffering and sorrow as great as anyone's,
    and I realised that the brokenness of this world
    grieved you as much as me.
You were there all along, sharing the hurt,
    weeping over everything that denies your love
    and frustrates your purpose,
    but you were there also to support and strengthen,
    reaching through the pain to share it and bear it,
    and finally to lead us through.
Remind me of that whenever life is hard and days are dark,
    and teach me, then above all times,
    to pray from the heart:
    'rescue me from evil'.
Amen.

Ponder

- Have you faced experiences that posed a serious challenge to your faith? What were these? How did you get through them?
- Are you awake to circumstances that might threaten or undermine your faith? How do you combat these?
- Do you expect God to safeguard you against the trials and difficulties of this world, or is your faith strong enough to take whatever life might throw at it?

Close

Living God,
I know my weakness all too well:
my lack of faith,
my limited courage,
my flawed commitment.
I know, should testing come,
that I will struggle to hold on,
my discipleship less secure than I would wish.
Protect me, then, from evil,
safeguard me from temptation,
and deliver me from times of trial,
through Jesus Christ my Lord.
Amen.

Day 25: Putting things into context

Approach

Living God,
   remind me today of your greatness and power,
   your will and purpose,
   and your grace and mercy,
   and may that knowledge shape who I am
   and all I do,
   today and always.
Amen.

Read

For the kingdom, the power and the glory are yours, now and for-evermore. Amen.
Matthew 6:13b; added in some ancient manuscripts only

Reflect

Have you ever watched a favourite film from which a scene has been cut? You sit there, taking it all in, only to realise suddenly that something is missing, what to you was an essential ingredient no longer there. The film still holds together – indeed, someone watching it for the first time would be oblivious to the omission – but to you it just doesn't feel quite right.

There was something of that feeling, I think, among those who read Matthew's version of the Lord's Prayer. It represented faithfully the words that Jesus had taught, but it wasn't quite the prayer they had become used to repeating. Why? Because just about every prayer used at the time would end with a doxology, an affirmation of faith, a statement summing up the sovereign nature of God, to whom the prayer was offered. And so it was that various copies of Matthew's Gospel appeared with a line added to the prayer: additional words that will be familiar to every Christian and many others today: 'For the kingdom, the power and the glory are yours, now and forevermore. Amen.'

Was that merely an arbitrary embellishment, a postscript added as an afterthought? I don't think so. It was included not just because the prayer *felt* incomplete but because those who prayed it felt it actually *was*. Possibly they believed Matthew had forgotten the exact words that Jesus used or perhaps they felt that this was the way Jesus expected us to conclude in prayer. Either way, the addition is important, for it sets the context not just for this prayer and for the Sermon on the Mount in general, but also for the whole of Jesus' life and ministry. He has spoken about God's kingdom and helping to bring it closer here on earth; he has referred to temptation and evil that might deflect us from the path of discipleship; he has touched on the need to align ourselves to God's will if we would truly see it done – and each of these are points we do well to remember. But there is a danger of us losing sight of the fact that though God's will may currently be frustrated, though his kingdom is not yet realised, and though temptation strikes and evil seems victorious, the future is secure, all things ultimately in his hands. The kingdom, power and glory are indeed his, now and always; he will not fail.

We can apply that further to everything Jesus has to say in the Sermon on the Mount, much of which can seem daunting, hopelessly beyond us. How can we love our enemies, go the extra mile, be salt and light to the world, overcome our self-centredness, and show works that correspond to our faith? The answer is, of course, that we can't. If it was down to us alone, we wouldn't have a hope of success or anywhere to turn for help. But we, like everything else, are finally in God's hands. He is able to use us beyond our every expectation and to forgive when we fail, patiently and lovingly moulding us into his people, however many times he needs to refashion the clay and start again. The kingdom, power and glory are his; so also, thank God, are we.

Pray

Lord,
    I feel overwhelmed sometimes,
    dwarfed by the problems that confront this world,
    by the forces of evil we're up against,
    by the trials and tragedies of so many,
    and by the things you ask and expect of me in response.
These consume my attention so that I see little else,
    rearing up at me, daunting and forbidding,
    destroying my faith that anything or anyone can change,
    least of all me.
I dwell on failure instead of success,
    defeat instead of victory,
    appalled by the scale of the obstacles that frustrate your will
    rather than amazed by the resources you offer
    to overcome them
    and the way you have so consistently worked over the years,
    bringing joy out of sorrow,
    hope out of despair,
    light out of darkness
    and life out of death.
Remind me again of who and what you are,
    of the great deeds you have done,
    of the promises you have given,
    of the things you are doing here and now.
Remind me that yours is the kingdom, the power and the glory;
    that you are the source of all that is
    and the arbiter of all that shall be;
    the Lord of heaven and earth,
    sovereign,
    exalted,
    enthroned in splendour and might.
Above all, remind me that what *I* cannot begin to achieve,
    you can accomplish beyond anything I might ever ask or imagine,
    and so may the only thing to overwhelm me as I go through life
    be a sense of your unfailing love,

your great mercy,
your awesome power
and your gracious purpose,
    through which all things will find their fulfilment in you.
Amen.

Ponder

- How often do you give God the praise and worship he deserves?
- Do you still have a sense of God's greatness and of all he is able to achieve?
- Do you feel powerless sometimes to make any contribution to God's kingdom, incapable of responding to his challenge? Do you wonder if anything can really ever be different? Are you focusing on your weakness or on God's strength?

Close

Lord of all,
    teach me to focus not on myself but on you,
    and may that put all else in perspective,
    so that I may happily leave every aspect of life
    safely in your hands.
In Christ's name I pray.
Amen.

Day 26: Treasures in heaven

Approach

Loving God,
    grant that all the blessings I have,
    the good things that surround me,
    may never cause me to overlook
    the treasure you have given me in Christ,
    the riches of life in abundance,
    eternal and ever-new.
Amen.

Read

Do not amass earthly treasures for yourselves, vulnerable to attack by moths or rust, or to thieves breaking in and making off with them. Instead accrue treasures in heaven, vulnerable neither to moths, rust nor larceny. For you can be sure of this; wherever your treasure is to be found, your heart will be found too.
Matthew 6:19-21

Reflect

On a freezing January afternoon in 1943, a ploughman by the name of Gordon Butcher uncovered an unusual-looking metal plate while out in the fields. Further investigation by his boss, Sydney Ford – the landowner and a collector of local antiquities – revealed a further 33 items, each of which found their way on to Ford's mantelpiece alongside other artefacts he'd collected over the years. Ford assumed they were made of pewter, but a visitor some years later realised differently. The items were in fact silver and dated back to Roman times, the whole collection – which was to become known as the Mildenhall Treasure – representing probably the most significant-ever discovery of its kind. Ford and

106

Butcher shared a reward of £2000 for their find – a not insignificant sum in those days, though a fraction of the cool £50,000 it was reckoned then to be worth. Today, its value is incalculable.

Not all treasures on earth, it seems, devalue with age. But that, of course, is to miss the point of what Jesus was saying in his words concerning treasures on earth and in heaven, for, however much that haul might be worth today, it ultimately proved of no lasting value whatsoever to the person who first owned it. As we often observe of worldly wealth, we can't take it with us. So it is now and so it has always been. Few would deny that the prospect of wealth is an attractive one. We'd all, I'm sure, like to see a little more in our pay packets, a growth in our investments, or a windfall to tide us over in early retirement, and there's nothing intrinsically wrong in any of these. Our mistake is if we see them as guaranteeing happiness, promising an end to our problems or cure to our ills. It may be a cliché to say that money doesn't buy us happiness, but it's true nonetheless. No price can be put on the gifts God offers us: peace, joy, hope, love, life, fulfilment. These cannot be bought, nor can they be hoarded away. They are to be received with thanks-giving and shared with similar gratitude, received afresh each day from God's outstretched hands. And with these gifts there's no question of not being able to take them with us, for death does not separate us from the riches he delights to bestow. On the contrary, it opens the way to experience them more fully and to receive the treasures he yet holds in store; treasures too wonderful for words to express – treasure in heaven!

Pray

Forgive me, Lord,
    for I'd forgotten how rich I was.
I looked at others,
    and saw what they earned,
    what they owned,
    and I was jealous,
    asking why *I* shouldn't have the same,

and, before I knew it,
instead of appreciating what I had,
I found myself dwelling on all I didn't have,
wanting more of this,
more of that,
more of everything.
Yet whatever I acquired, I coveted something extra,
possessions failing to satisfy as I'd expected,
pleasing enough for a moment,
but their shine soon fading.
I'd lost sight, Lord, of what's truly of value:
joy,
peace,
hope,
love;
the knowledge that I'm valued by you,
accepted for what I am;
the assurance of your forgiveness;
the daily experience of your presence,
by my side
and deep within.
There's no price I can put on those,
for their worth is beyond measure,
too wonderful for words,
yet you offer them freely,
not just now but for all eternity.
Save me, then, from chasing after illusory happiness,
from attempting to fill my life with what can never truly fulfil.
Teach me simply to look to you
and to open my heart to your grace,
recognising that you have blessed me in abundance –
that I am rich indeed.
Amen.

Ponder

- How much store do you set on possessions? How important to you are the comforts of this life? What is your heart most set on?
- How much time do you invest in securing treasure in heaven as opposed to riches on earth?
- Which spiritual treasures do you value most? How far is it possible, as Jesus seems to suggest, to store up such treasures for ourselves? What do you think he meant?

Close

Gracious God,
   remind me again of the privilege of knowing you,
   the joy of loving you
   and the enrichment of serving you –
   the priceless treasure of experiencing
   your gracious presence each day;
   new life now and for all eternity.
Amen.

Day 27: Seeing the light

Approach

Lord Jesus Christ,
   Light of the world,
   shine on me,
   shine in me,
   shine through me,
   and so bring honour to your name.
Amen.

Read

The eye acts as a lantern for the whole body. If, then, it is sound, every part of the body will be illumined; but if there is something wrong with it, then you will be plunged into darkness. If what should shed light in you in fact brings only darkness, how total that darkness will be!
Matthew 6:22-23

Reflect

A little knowledge, so they say, is a dangerous thing, and, not long ago, I was to discover the truth of that first-hand. A light-fitting needed replacing in our hallway, and, since the job seemed straightforward enough, I decided to have a stab at it myself. It seemed somewhat less uncomplicated once I removed the ceiling rose and uncovered a tangled mass of wires, many more than I had expected to find and none of them colour-coded. 'Never mind,' I thought, 'I can manage. If I note carefully where each wire is placed as I disconnect it, there should be no problem connecting them all again afterwards.' That, at least, was the theory, but when I finally reassembled the fitting and flicked the light switch, I looked up in anticipation only to see . . . nothing. For some reason, power was obviously not getting through. 'A light's come on out here!' called my wife from the kitchen. 'And in here!' shouted my son from the dining room. 'All very strange,' I thought. 'What on earth's going on!' Half an hour later, and working by torchlight as night descended, I was still no further forward, every light coming on in the house, it seemed, except the one that was meant to. It was time, I decided, to call in an electrician, and within a few minutes of his arrival the job was done.

Was my attempt at wiring dangerous? I'm not sure, but it certainly could have been. The trouble with a little knowledge is that we tend to think we know more than we do. Indeed, often the less we understand the more likely we are to imagine that we know it all. That, more or less, is what Jesus was warning of in his words concerning light and darkness, though he had one thing especially in mind: our knowledge of God. There is no error potentially more disastrous, he says, than believing we see God when we don't; than thinking our grasp of spiritual realities is sure when in fact it is flimsy; than assuming we have understood what God wishes, what discipleship entails and what faith means when in fact we've barely begun to glimpse such things at all. Why? Because the illusion blinds us to our innermost needs, lulling us into a naïve complacency, a distorted picture of God.

Can that happen to us? Undoubtedly. Whether or not it actually applies to you is not for me or anyone else to say, but none of us is immune from mistaking a superficial knowledge of God for something deeper, a nominal faith for genuine commitment. The wise Christian is one who is not only always learning but who is also aware that our knowledge is at best partial, constantly needing to be open to fresh insights, to be stretched, challenged and even revised in the light of daily experience. Forget that, and though we may believe we've seen the light, we may inadvertently be walking deeper and deeper into darkness.

Pray

It was a shock, Lord.
I thought I knew him inside out,
    understanding, as well as any, what made him tick,
    the sort of person he was.
But he took me by surprise,
    showing a side to his character I never knew existed,
    qualities I wouldn't have believed possible,
    depths I hadn't even dreamt of.
The mistake was mine, of course.
To presume, even for a moment, that I could know
    all there was to know,
    grasp the whole truth rather than just a fraction,
    was foolish of me,
    quite wrong.
    for what I thought was comprehension
    actually blinded me to reality,
    obscuring what I could and would have seen
    if only I'd been open to what was there before me.
Lord,
    save me from doing the same with you,
    from mistakenly believing my faith is complete,
    my knowledge of you total.
Prevent me from limiting what you are
    to what I conceive you to be,
    from restricting the way you can shape my life
    to the way I expect you to work,
    from confusing my partial grasp of your grace
    with the full wonder of the gospel.
Keep me always open to fresh insights and deeper understanding,
    to a richer and fuller revelation of truth.
Whatever light I have glimpsed,
    remind me that there is more to break through.
Open my eyes, then, each day to see and know you better,
    until that time when I enter into the radiance of your presence
    and meet you face to face.
Amen.

Ponder

- Are there times when what you have assumed to be true has in fact blinded you to the truth?
- Has this been the case sometimes in your understanding and experience of God?
- Are you still open to your picture of God and perception of faith being broadened, even if it means accepting you have been wrong about some things up to now?

Close

Living God,
    open not only my eyes
    but also my mind,
    my heart,
    and my soul
    to your gracious love,
    your redeeming power
    and your sovereign purpose.
Give me insight, faith and understanding,
    so that I may glimpse your hand at work
    in every aspect of life
    and discern your presence
    every moment of every day.
Amen.

Day 28: Decision time

Approach

Almighty God,
    teach me what it means to love you,
    what it takes to follow you
    and what it costs to serve you,
    and help me to stay true when testing comes,
    choosing your way and walking it faithfully
    with all my heart and mind and soul.
Amen.

Read

It is impossible for people to serve two masters, for they will either hate the one and love the other, or cling to the one and spurn the other. You cannot simultaneously serve God and this world.
Matthew 6:24

Reflect

Have you ever been pulled two ways at the same time? Of course you have. It can happen among friends, for example, one wanting us to do this and another to do that; somehow we must decide which to please and which to disappoint. It can happen also within a family, nowhere more dramatically than in a tug-of-love situation where a child is torn between each parent, wanting to be with both but having to choose or accept choices between one or the other. Situations such as these give us some insight into what Jesus was saying concerning serving two masters, but they only scratch the surface, for, of course, we can, and often do, offer our loyalty to more than one person in a variety of circumstances. It may not always be easy, but we try to keep a balance between all kinds of relationships, staying as true as possible to all concerned.

An analogy that perhaps brings us closer to what Jesus had in mind might be in the workplace. Imagine that one of your superiors instructs you to focus on a certain piece of work at all costs, giving it priority over everything else, only for another superior, with equal authority, to issue a counter-instruction telling you to forget the first job and concentrate instead on a completely different task. Clearly that can't be done; something has to give. And that, says Jesus, is what sometimes happens in discipleship. It's not that faith and life, God and the world are constantly in conflict; far from it – after all, the world is God's gift reflecting, for all its blemishes, his love and purpose. Yet on occasions, nonetheless, discipleship leads to a conflict of interests, a clash of cultures, calling us to decide between God's way and the way of the world, between self-interest and the honouring of his will. There is no half-way house at such moments, no comfortable compromise that keeps all parties happy, allowing us to sidestep the challenge. We need to be clear about where our allegiance lies if we are successfully to meet the challenge they bring.

When serving God involves self-denial and sacrifice, putting his will and the good of others before your own, which way will you take? When life offers opportunities that entail compromising your convictions, sacrificing your principles, how will you react? When you're faced by a straight choice between a demanding way that you know to be right and an easy way that you know to be wrong, which will you choose: the challenging option or the path of least resistance? It's tempting to imagine sometimes that we can play it both ways, steer a middle course that gives us the best of both worlds, but the warning of Jesus is clear. Attempt to do that and instead of having a foot in both camps we may end up without a foot in either.

Pray

I thought I'd decided, Lord,
    committed myself irrevocably to your service,
    without reserve or qualification,
    but I see now I was wrong.
When faith involved sacrifice,
    putting you first and self second,
    I realised I was hedging my bets,
    serving you when it suited
    but determined to serve my own ends also.
I imagined I could marry the two,
    stay faithful to you, yet leave space for me,
    and I was right, some of the time,
    there being no clash of interests,
    no reason not to savour the joys of this world
    alongside the blessings of heaven.
But occasionally it was different,
    your call involving choices –
    stark,
    demanding,
    costly;
    the challenge to give and go on giving,
    to say no to compromise,
    to stand up for justice, against the odds,
    to speak out for faith where few would listen –
    choices I'd rather not make,
    challenges I'd no wish to face.
So I tried steering a middle course,
    a path between the two,
    only to find I achieved nothing,
    pleasing neither you nor me.
Forgive me,
    and help me to decide where my priorities lie.
Teach me to put you first, above all else,
    renouncing whatever may keep me from your side
    or prevent me from following your way.

Whenever choices must be made,
    Lord, help me to make them,
    staying faithful to you, come what may.
Amen.

Ponder

- In what areas of life have you felt a clash between what you want and what you believe God is asking?
- Are you facing circumstances now in which your loyalties are divided? Have you compromised what you believe rather than prejudice your prospects in any way?
- Are there ways in which you are still trying to keep a foot in both camps?

Close

Sovereign God,
    save me from offering half-hearted discipleship,
    compromised commitment,
    divided loyalty,
    vacillating service.
Teach me to offer my all to you
    as surely as you offered your all to me in Christ.
In his name I pray.
Amen.

Day 29: Glimpses of God

Approach

Creator God,
> open my eyes to glimpse something of you in the miracle of life,
> the beauty of this earth
> and the vastness of the universe.

May these speak to me of your purpose,
> your love
> and your greatness,
> and lead me into a deeper understanding
> of who and what you are,
> through Jesus Christ my Lord.

Amen.

Read

So then, I tell you straight, do not vex yourself about life, what you will eat or drink, and do not worry about what you might clothe yourselves with. Is not life more than food, and the body more than clothing? Observe the birds flying about you; they do not sow, harvest or hoard reserves in barns, but your heavenly Father feeds them. Are you not much more valuable than they? Which of you by brooding can extend your lifespan by even one hour? So then, why do you fret over the outfits you're going to wear? See how the wild flowers grow, pay heed to them. They do not labour or weave, yet I can assure you that not even Solomon in all his grandeur was decked out like one of these. If God clothes the grass of the field like this – grass that though here today, tomorrow will be tossed on to a bonfire – will he not clothe you all the more richly, you of such little faith? So then, no more of this worrying, these plaintive cries of 'What shall I eat . . . what can I drink . . . what can I wear?' It is the Gentiles who crave such things as these; your Father in heaven is well aware of what you

need. But seek first the kingdom and the righteousness of God, and you will be given everything else you need in addition.
Matthew 6:25-33

Reflect

Take a tour of any stately home and you will almost certainly come across several pictures depicting scenes purporting to represent ancient Rome, Tuscany or Greece. They present enchanting and unforgettable images, but the majority of these, so I'm told, derive from the artists' imagination rather than any specific place. Temples, vistas, animals, mountains and streams have been arbitrarily added to create an idealised scene, one that corresponds to how the artist in question believed things should have looked rather than how they actually did.

As Christians, we can do something very similar when it comes to nature, substituting an idealised picture for the real thing. Hymn-writers, poets, apologists and many others have held up the natural world as pointing conclusively to God, revealing his love, care and purpose for all, ostensibly beyond dispute. I would not question for a moment that nature can indeed speak of God. The sky at night, the might of the ocean, the peacefulness of a wood or meadow, the grandeur of a view from a mountaintop can all powerfully convey an awareness of the divine, what the theologian Rudolf Otto once termed 'the idea of the holy'. But alongside its beauty, nature also has its ugly side, red in tooth and claw; what we might term the law of the jungle or the survival of the fittest. We are part of an imperfect world in which God's will is as much frustrated as fulfilled, and in which much speaks of the forces of chaos and confusion rather than of order and a loving purpose.

We cannot prove the existence of God from the natural world, and to attempt to do so does no service to anyone, discrediting rather than promoting the gospel. Yet, to the eye of faith, there is enough around us, even in things as simple as a flower bursting into bloom or a bird pecking at seed, to speak to us of the one who lies behind it all; the hand of God that not only fashioned the universe but also reaches out afresh each day, providing the essentials of life and the promise of life to come. Despite all that spoils and destroys, denies and disfigures, we can catch sight around us of an architect's design, a Creator's power and a sovereign purpose.

'Observe the birds flying about you,' says Jesus. 'See how the wild flowers grow, pay heed to them.' And to those we could add so much more. These do not provide proof of God, nor give us the whole truth about him, but they give us a glimpse of the one who loves us more than we can imagine and who yearns, in the fullness of time, in a new earth and heaven, to shower us with blessings beyond measure.

Pray

It's easy to romanticise, Lord,
    to gush about all things bright and beautiful,
    all creatures great and small,
    as though anyone need only look at these,
    and, if they have any sense whatsoever,
    they will bow down in worship,
    fall to their knees in adoration,
    acknowledging you as the living God,
    Creator of all.
But it's not that simple,
    for alongside the good there's the bad,
    beside the lovely, the ugly –
    viruses, germs and diseases,
    famine and natural disaster,
    all manner of pain and suffering hidden from view –
    and though some of that may be down to us,
    to human ignorance, wilfulness or folly,
    most is out of our hands,
    impossible to control,
    harder still to understand.

Yet if much confuses,
   much also inspires.
If much confounds,
   much also illuminates.
If much conceals,
   much also speaks of your hand at work,
   your creative purpose,
   your intricate design.
Lord,
   I know that all creation groans together,
   eagerly awaiting its redemption in Christ,
   so any picture I may gain from it is necessarily imperfect,
   incomplete,
   but I thank you for those things
   that nevertheless speak to me of you,
   stirring the spirit,
   touching the heart
   and reinforcing faith
   that your love will ultimately perfect all things,
   leading them to their fulfilment in you.
Open my eyes more fully to whatever may help me glimpse you
   better,
   so that trust may grow
   and faith be deepened.
In Christ's name I pray.
Amen.

Ponder

- What in the natural world speaks to you of God?
- What things in the natural world challenge your faith in God?
- What are the strengths and weaknesses of drawing analogies
  with God from the world around us?

Close

Awesome God,
    open my eyes to everything around me,
    to the wonder of this world you have given,
    and through it all help me to hear your voice
    and respond to your call.
Amen.

Day 30: One day at a time

Approach

Sovereign God,
 take this day,
 this hour,
 this moment,
 and help me to live each to the full,
 knowing that you are here with me now
 as you are with me always.
Amen.

Read

So do not brood about tomorrow; you can be sure it will bring its sufficient share of difficulties. Take one day at a time, for each has enough problems of its own.
Matthew 6:34

Reflect

'Cheer up,' he said, 'it may never happen!' And, of course, he was right. How often do we spend days, weeks, even months worrying about some eventuality that ultimately never transpires. As a result, we end up looking back ruefully, regretting the happiness and peace of mind we could have enjoyed if only we had been able to put our anxiety to one side. Conversely, there are times when trouble and tragedy strike unexpectedly. 'Who knows what tomorrow might bring?' the saying goes, and sometimes we must be thankful that we don't, for if we did know in advance we'd find the knowledge hard to cope with. For all kinds of reasons, the tried and trusted advice 'one day at a time' is well worth following. Life is too short to waste it ruminating on what has been or what might be. Yet we all do it, don't we? We can't help regretting past mistakes, thinking if only we'd done such and such, then things would be very different. Or we look back nostalgically to the good old days, convinced that things were so much better then than now.

With the future the temptation is even stronger. We plan ahead for holidays, special occasions, children, career, retirement, and so much else, eagerly anticipating what these might bring, or we worry about what might happen, turning over a host of possibilities in our minds and wondering how we might cope if they come about. Yet, as Jesus so rightly says, 'Which of us by worrying can add even a fraction to our height?' 'Do not brood about what tomorrow might bring,' he tells us, each day has enough problems of its own; which, in somewhat sombre form, reiterates the message of Psalm 118: 'This is the day the Lord has made. Let us rejoice and be glad in it.' It's a message we've all heard before in one form or another, but while it's one of the easiest to understand it's one of the hardest to apply. Are you still fretting over the past, still brooding about tomorrow? If so, it's time to remind yourself once again, and to keep on reminding yourself until it finally sinks home: 'One day at a time'.

Pray

'Take things as they come,' he said.
'One day,
   one moment,
   at a time.'
And I knew it made sense, Lord;
   that it's foolish to fret,
   for what's done is done
   and what must be will be,
   yet I can't help dwelling sometimes on the past
   and brooding on the future:
   the things I should have done,
   and those I *have* done;
   the things I hope will come,
   and those that *might* come.
I saw the man rushed to hospital
   and I thought that one day it could be me.

I saw the patients in the nursing home
    and I feared that one day it *will* be me.
I saw the baby in the photo,
    and I reflected that one day, not so long ago, it *was* me.
Times gone by,
    times to come,
    and both scare me in their way,
    for one's over,
    lost for ever,
    and the other lies in wait,
    no knowing what it might bring,
    for good or ill.
But I know one thing, Lord;
    remind me of that:
    the truth that your love endures for ever,
    the same yesterday, today and tomorrow.
Teach me, then, that whatever life may bring
    you will be with me in it,
    there by my side to strengthen,
    sustain,
    succour
    and support.
In that knowledge may I put all in your hands,
    and live each moment as your gift
    in grateful praise
    and joyful service.
Amen.

Ponder

- How often do you stop and simply enjoy the present moment?
- How often do you make a point of thanking God for it?
- Do you spend too much time brooding over the past or worrying about the future? Is it time you changed your approach to life?

Close

God of all,
    save me from brooding over the past
    or worrying about the future;
    from being preoccupied by regrets
    or troubled by what might happen.
Teach me instead to celebrate the present;
    to live each day as it comes,
    receiving it as your gift
    and meeting whatever it brings,
    for good or ill,
    in your strength
    and to your glory.
Amen.

Day 31: Who are we to judge?

Approach

Eternal God,
    unfold to me the enormity of your love,
    the magnitude of your care,
    the scale of your mercy
    and the vastness of your grace.
Teach me more of who and what you are,
    so that I may deal with others
    as you have dealt with me.
Amen.

Read

If you don't want to be judged, don't sit in judgement on others, for you will be judged by the same yardstick, evaluated according to the evaluation you yourself employ. How is it that you notice a piece of sawdust in your neighbour's eye, yet overlook the plank in your own? How can you offer to take the fragment out of your neighbour's eye while that great beam of wood is still sticking out of yours? What a hypocrite you are! If only you were to remove the beam from your own eye you'd have a much clearer picture of that speck troubling your neighbour.
Matthew 7:1-5

Reflect

'If you don't want to be judged, don't sit in judgement on others' – that idea is developed in some detail in the Sermon on the Mount, so it was clearly important in the thinking of Jesus. We find it repeated elsewhere in the Scriptures, not least in the Epistle of James, where it could justifiably be said to comprise the key theme of the letter. We may reasonably conclude, therefore, that

127

refusing to judge others should be a fundamental characteristic of the Christian life, something that should mark out all who claim to follow Jesus. But is that so? I suspect, sadly, that the opposite is nearer the mark. If you wish to uncover examples of bigotry, narrow-mindedness, intolerance, or negative and hypercritical attitudes, then the Church is as good a place to start looking as any. The problem is that religion, like politics, arouses strong feelings, even passions. Beliefs become so precious to those who hold them, convictions so entrenched, that to have anyone question them is seen not just as a personal affront but also as an attack on truth and morality. Too easily we confuse our relative understanding of good and evil, right and wrong, with absolute reality, with God himself. It is a disastrous mistake with potentially lethal consequences. Witness the wars that have been fought in the name of religion, the persecution of Catholics by Protestants and Protestants by Catholics across the centuries, all manner of atrocities carried out across the world in the name of the gospel, not to mention divisions that still scar the Church today. If these, though, are the large-scale manifestations of judgemental attitudes, there are many smaller but equally damaging consequences. How easily we pass judgement on sections in society whose ways differ to our own; how often we condemn people in our daily relationships on the basis of partial and often misinterpreted evidence; how frequently we criticise in others the very faults and weaknesses that are infinitely more apparent in ourselves, seeing the speck of sawdust in someone's eye while overlooking the beam in our own.

As Christians we find it particularly hard not to judge, because we believe we have certain standards that we need to safeguard, a way of life that we must stay true to if we are to honour Christ, and we are afraid that if we blur the edges, then moral chaos may follow. Yet, if we could but see it, this, once again, is making the cardinal mistake of setting ourselves up as God. Certainly, we must live as we believe he calls us to, but we must *not* impose on others the requirement to do the same. We are brought back ultimately to Jesus' command to love, the one commandment that we should focus on above all others. If only we as Christians could do just that, putting the time we spend in judging others into loving them instead, this world would be an infinitely happier place, and the cause of Christ would be advanced beyond anything we might imagine.

Pray

I can't help judging sometimes, Lord.
I need to make up my mind
    about the rights and wrongs of a situation,
    about people's actions and the motives behind them,
    about whether things are acceptable or unacceptable,
    good or evil.
If I didn't do that I'd be weak, foolish, naïve,
    lacking in principles or conviction,
    easy prey for the unscrupulous.
It goes wider than that, though,
    for there are times too when, as a society,
    we need to pass judgement,
    literally,
    sentencing those who break the law,
    who hurt, destroy, wound or kill,
    for how else can we safeguard the well-being of all?
So it doesn't come easily, understanding these words of yours,
    recognising how they might apply to daily life,
    to this world as we know it.
Yet I can see clearly enough
    that it's one thing to believe an action is wrong,
    quite another to set myself up as sole judge and jury;
    one thing to have reservations about someone's words or actions,
    altogether different to write them off entirely.
You do not say there's no such thing as judgement,
    still less play down the distinction between good or evil,
    but what you do say is that it's not for me
    to pronounce the final verdict;

that is down to you alone.
Save me, then, from narrow judgemental attitudes,
    from the assumption that I am right and others are wrong.
Save me from seeing the faults in others
    but being blind to those within myself.
Give me a spirit that builds people up
    rather than tears them down;
    that discerns the good
    rather than dwells on the bad;
    that brings out the best
    rather than highlights the worst.
Instead of passing judgement on others, teach me to love
    just as you have so wonderfully and unreservedly loved me,
    through Jesus Christ my Lord.
Amen.

Ponder

- Are there ways in which you are guilty of being judgemental?
- How do you think others might judge you?
- Are there areas in which the Church comes across as narrow, intolerant, self-righteous and holier-than-thou? Does it need to moderate its views according to changing times, or simply to adapt the way it presents its message?

Close

Gracious God,
    for your blessing beyond deserving,
    your mercy beyond all reason
    and your love that knows no bounds,
    receive my praise
    and help me to show my gratitude
    by showing the same compassion in my dealings with others
    that you have shown to me.
Amen.

Day 32: A time and place for everything

Approach

Almighty God,
    show me how and where to work for you,
    to love for you
    and to live for you,
    through Jesus Christ my Lord.
Amen.

Read

Do not toss what is sacred to the dogs, or feed pearls to swine, for they will simply stamp all over them or turn and attack you.
Matthew 7:6

Reflect

I could barely conceal my disappointment as we looked out together at the view. 'Isn't it wonderful?' I said. 'Have you ever seen anywhere more beautiful?' But clearly my companion thought otherwise. 'It's all right,' she said, 'if you like that sort of thing.' I'd been building up the place throughout our walk, extolling its loveliness, for to me it was little short of paradise, but to my friend, though it was pleasant enough, it was nothing special, nothing to write home about. No doubt we've all had similar experiences, times when we've desperately wanted to share something precious to us, yet failed to discover the response we'd hoped for. It might be a piece of music, a poem, book or film, an interest or hobby, a painting, photograph or sculpture, the song of a bird or sound of the sea – these things and countless others can capture our imagination such that we are breathless with wonder, yet leave another cold. So often, as the old saying has it, 'beauty is in the eye of the beholder'.

131

There is something of this idea, I think, behind the words of Jesus concerning pearls before swine and giving what is holy to dogs. The verse is disturbing, isn't it, sitting awkwardly with everything we believe about Jesus and the Christian way of life, but in fact the language here is deliberately chosen as a sort of shock tactic, a commonly used teaching device among Jewish rabbis. Through putting things so bluntly and colourfully, the listener – or in our case, reader – is prompted to sit up, take notice and ask what these words are all about. Jesus, in other words, is grabbing our attention. But why? What is the point he is trying to make? Those who have tried to share their faith will, I suspect, have at least an inkling, for they will have shared also the frustration and disappointment I talked about earlier. What is good news to us, the wonderfully exciting message of God's love in Christ, to another can seem old hat, dull as dishwater, of no interest whatsoever. More often than not, our attempts at witnessing to our faith meet with apathy and indifference, few people if any wanting to listen. Is this to say we are the elite, looking down on others as spiritual plebeians? Not at all. It is to recognise rather that we are all different, and that God speaks to people in his own way and time. Some may respond to another person, another approach. Some, for all kinds of reasons, may not be ready to listen at a given moment, whereas at another point in their life they might be highly receptive. Others may need time to ponder and reflect, weighing up the issues concerned before they are willing to commit themselves. And so we could go on. The thrust of Jesus' words, as I understand them, is that we should not persist in pushing something, not even the message of the gospel, where it is not wanted. Not only will that be a waste of our time, but it may also do more harm than good. I cannot persuade you that a piece of music, painting or poem is better than any other; it's all a matter of personal perspective. Neither can I or anyone else persuade somebody that committing their life to Christ is the best decision they can ever take. We need to share, yes, but we need also to recognise that faith finally is down to God.

Pray

I should have stopped, Lord, shouldn't I –
    realised that enough was enough?
But instead I ploughed on regardless,
    convinced that I could make a difference.
I spoke because I wanted to make you known –
    to share my faith and communicate your love –
    but the blank eyes and wrinkled brow
    should have told me to let go,
    to realise that the time wasn't right,
    the person not ready,
    the stage not set.
I did it again,
    speaking this time because I thought I had to,
    believing it my duty to witness to you and declare your name,
    but the flashing eyes and narrowed brow
    should have warned me off,
    telling me that the moment was wrong,
    the person hostile,
    the soil infertile.
I meant well,
    and was right to try,
    but who knows the harm I've done,
    the damage I've caused,
    by outstaying my welcome,
    carrying on where I wasn't wanted.
Alongside eagerness and enthusiasm, Lord,
    give me sensitivity.
Alongside obedience to your word,
    give me discernment.
Teach me when to speak
    and when to keep silent;
    what to say
    and what is best left unspoken.
Teach me that there's a time and place for everything,
    and help me to know when each one is.
Amen.

Ponder

- Have you ever tried arguing somebody into faith? What was the result?
- Was there a time when you were hostile to or disinterested in the gospel? How would you have reacted if someone had 'preached' at you then? What does this suggest to you about sharing your faith?
- How would you gauge the right time and place to witness to Christ?

Close

Sovereign God,
    speak to me
    and teach me when to speak for you.
Give me sensitivity to all –
    and so may I say the right words
    in the right way
    for the right people
    at the right moment
    to the glory of your name
    and the growth of your kingdom.
Amen.

Day 33: Ask, seek, knock

Approach

Living God,
   direct my thinking,
   my longing,
   my seeking
   and my finding,
   that I may live in you
   and you in me,
   through Jesus Christ my Lord.
Amen.

Read

Ask, and you will receive; seek, and you will find what you're looking for; knock, and the door will be thrown open. For whoever asks receives, and whoever searches finds, and to whoever knocks, the door will be opened. Would any among you, should your child ask for bread, give a stone? Or if asked for a fish, would you give a snake? If then, you who are flawed know how to give good gifts to your children, how much more will your heavenly Father give good things to those who ask him!
Matthew 7:7-11

Reflect

If ever the danger of taking Scripture out of context was apparent, it can surely be nowhere clearer than in the first few words of our passage today: 'Ask, and you will receive'. Many have used those words to argue that we need only to request something with sufficient faith and it will be ours. Imagine the consequences were that actually so: God would be at our beck and call, subject to whatever whim happened to take our fancy. That would make a mockery of everything we believe, for instead of us looking to do his will, we would be expecting him to do ours. It would be a recipe for chaos and disaster, the prospect unthinkable.

A closer look at the passage in which these words are set, however, reveals that this interpretation is very far from what Jesus had in mind. His instruction to ask is part of a wider instruction to ask, seek and knock, and needs to be understood in the still wider context of the sermon as a whole. What was it Jesus said earlier? Do not ask what you will eat, drink or wear, for God knows that we need such things already. Rather, we should seek first – and above all else – his kingdom and his righteousness. The same message comes across in his words on treasures on earth and in heaven, and yet again in his challenge to serve either God or this world, not both. In other words, it is clearly nonsense to interpret the opening words of Matthew 7:7 as meaning we need only ask for something in faith to receive it. We have no blank cheque here or offer of *carte-blanche*. Instead, Jesus is driving home the point that the blessings of heaven – true blessings – are open to all. Yes, God delights to bless us in all kinds of other ways too, but that doesn't mean we can ask him for a nice house, new car or good job. To believe that is to slip perilously close to the prosperity gospel we talked about earlier in relation to daily bread, impossible to reconcile with the plight of countless people, committed Christians among them, across the world. Too often and too easily as Christians we turn prayer, and even faith itself, into a kind of wish-fulfilment exercise, imagining that commitment will somehow guarantee that everything in life will come up smelling of roses. If we do that, we simply have not read the gospel, with its repeated emphasis on the cost of discipleship and the inverted values of God's kingdom.

Lobby God with a list of personal demands and there's no knowing what his response might be, whether he either should or will grant them. Ask, though, for lasting treasure, search for true fulfilment, knock at the door of his kingdom, yearning to be part of it, and, make no mistake, he will delight to hear and answer.

Pray

'Help me,' I prayed.
'Take away this problem.'
'Provide those funds.'
'Grant that job.'
In these, and a host of other ways, Lord,
    I've come to you in prayer,
    asking for first this,
    then that –
    as though you are a blank cheque,
    a guarantee card assuring that I will secure
    whatever blessing I seek.
But it's not like that, is it?
You *may* say yes, of course –
    indeed, you often do –
    but you may equally say no,
    faith not a promise of earthly comfort
    but of heavenly blessing.
You want me to ask, certainly,
    to seek
    and to knock at the door,
    but you've made clear also
    what the object of my asking should be,
    the goal of my search,
    the purpose of my knocking –
    each concerned with your kingdom
    and your righteousness,
    with leading me closer to you,
    and teaching me more of your way
    so that I might know and serve you better.
I'll still ask as I used to, Lord,
    still seek your blessing in the daily affairs of life,
    for I need your guidance and help so much,
    but teach me also and especially to ask for what really matters,
    to search for eternal riches,
    to knock at the gates of life in all its fullness,

knowing that you will be there,
waiting to fling them open and welcome me in.
Amen.

Ponder

- What sort of requests characterise your prayer life?
- How often, and how sincerely, do you ask God to deepen and enrich your faith? What steps do you take to help him answer that prayer? Do you play your part or leave it all to him?
- Are you puzzled that God doesn't seem to have answered certain of your prayers? Have you been praying for the right thing? Have you understood what prayer is all about?

Close

Living God,
before I ask for anything,
teach me what to ask for;
before I seek your blessing,
teach me what that means;
before I presume to knock,
teach me which door to choose.
Guide me in your ways,
through Jesus Christ my Lord.
Amen.

Day 34: Do as you would be done by

Approach

Gracious God,
　　I would live for you,
　　love like you,
　　trust in you
　　and walk with you.
Teach me, then, your way
　　and equip me to follow it,
　　to your glory.
Amen.

Read

In everything do as you would be done by; for this sums up what the law and the prophets are all about.
Matthew 7:12

Reflect

Do as you would be done by. It's a well-known and eminently sensible saying, isn't it? And, like so many often-used aphorisms, it dates right back to biblical times, in this case to the words of Jesus in the Sermon on the Mount. The adage, in fact, is an extension of what Jesus had taught just a little earlier concerning forgiveness; namely, that we will be shown mercy in proportion to the mercy we are willing to show. Here, however, the horizon is widened to include every aspect of behaviour: act towards others, says Jesus, exactly as you would have them act towards you.

　　If only people followed that precept, what a different world it would be; how much suffering and sorrow, hatred and violence we would be spared and how much more happiness and harmony, friendship and contentment would be shared. If only, if only. It is not enough, though, simply to shrug our shoulders in regret, grieving over what might have been, for Jesus puts the onus on each of us to take the initiative in helping vision become reality. Effectively, what he asks of us is the flipside to loving our enemies, going the extra mile and turning the other cheek, for his challenge is to do to others not what they *actually* do to us – in other words, an eye for an eye and a tooth for a tooth – but what, ideally, we would *like* them to do. We are called to love, even though we are not loved; to forgive, even though we are not forgiven; to give, even though we do not receive; to serve, even though no service is offered in return; and so we could go on. No wonder Jesus understands this little maxim as a summary of the law and the prophets, for it provides us with a perfect synopsis of Christian ethics. Nothing could be simpler yet more profound, so apparently straightforward yet having such far-reaching consequences.

The ball is in our court. If we wait for others to change, we will probably wait a lifetime. We may wait a lifetime anyway, even if we make the first move, but that's not the point. If there is to be any prospect of change, any possibility of God's kingdom coming a little closer here on earth, then it needs you and me, and all who confess the name of Christ, to do what we can, no matter how small, to help make a difference. If *we* don't lead the way, why should anyone follow?

Pray

Nice one, Lord!
You've hit the nail on the head,
    you're summary of the law and the prophets
    encapsulating all I try to live by:
    doing to others as I've had done to me.
That's right, isn't it?
Of course it is . . .
    what else could you mean?

OK, if someone wrongs me, I'll look to get even,
    but that's different, isn't it? –
    a question of simple justice.
If someone picks a fight,
    starts a quarrel,
    then of course they get what's coming to them.
All right,
    so perhaps occasionally I'm the transgressor –
    acting unkindly,
    doing what you'd rather I didn't –
    but if so there'll be good reason, you can be sure of that,
    such behaviour the exception rather than the norm.
It's a matter of give and take, I suppose –
    I'll scratch their back if they scratch mine:
    that's what you're after, Lord, I assume.
What's that?
I've got it wrong?
Surely not!
You can't mean do to others what I'd *have* done to me
    instead of what I've *had* done!
You *do*, don't you!
You really want me to put others first and self second!
But that's such a huge gamble,
    such a massive leap of faith!
And who can say where it all might lead?
I thought I'd understood,
    but I hadn't,
    I *still* haven't –
    my head in a spin as I struggle to take it in,
    let alone accept and follow.
I need help, Lord,
    your Spirit within me,
    for I can't do it alone,
    even should I wish to.
Give me the strength I need,
    the courage and commitment to deal with others your way,

as you say,
recognising that, costly though it may seem,
it is no more so –
indeed, far less –
than the way you have dealt with me in Christ.
Amen.

Ponder

- Is your natural reaction when hurt by someone to hurt them back? Do you treat others as they treat you, or as you *wish* they treated you?
- Are there areas in your daily relationships where you are conscious of failing to do as you would be done by? Are you ready to respond to the challenge of Jesus, and to amend your behaviour?
- Are you caught up in a spiral of tit-for-tat? Is it time you broke the cycle by putting the words of Jesus into practice?

Close

Gracious God,
    you gave your all for me in Christ,
    loving me before I ever loved you,
    accepting me before I ever thought of responding.
Teach me to show the same love,
    the same acceptance,
    the same willingness to give and go on giving,
    and so may your will be done here on earth
    as it is in heaven.
Amen.

Day 35: The wide and narrow gates

Approach

Sovereign God,
    guide me now as I read your word.
    May it speak afresh
    and offer guidance for daily life:
    lighting my path
    and directing my footsteps
    so that, in all things, I may walk with Christ.
Amen.

Read

Proceed through the narrow gate. Many choose the wide gate instead, but that path leads only to ruin. By contrast, the path that leads to life is straight and narrow, and is found by just a handful. *Matthew 7:13-14*

Reflect

A while back I had an unpleasant shock – almost literally. I went upstairs to my study, and found my cordless telephone gently smouldering, a column of smoke rising ominously from the base unit and a smell of burning plastic filling the room. Had I been a minute or two later, the whole house could easily have gone up in flames, but thankfully I had sufficient time to rush downstairs, turn the power off, and alert the electrician – who was working at the time on rewiring the kitchen – to the situation. The cause of the problem turned out to be surprisingly simple. A single wire, still sheathed, had become crushed against the metal plate within the oven socket, causing a small, but potentially devastating, residual current to leak through the insulation and feed up the telephone line, looking to earth itself along the path of least resistance.

143

What has that to do, you may ask, with the words of Jesus concerning the wide and narrow gates? Unlikely as it may seem, it says a great deal. You see, talk about two ways is all very well, but it means very little unless we understand what those two ways involve. Speaking generally, we might say Jesus is contrasting *his* way – the path of the cross – to the way of the world, but what does that mean in practice? My rogue electric current has the answer, for we share with it a tendency to take the way of least resistance. We prefer to go along with the world rather than make a stand of principle, to go for a quick fix rather than invest time and effort in securing a lasting solution, to enjoy an easy life rather than one that makes uncomfortable demands upon us. In short, we prefer self-service to serving others, self-interest to altruism, self-indulgence to sacrificial discipleship. Confronted by choices in life, nine times out of ten we will opt for the path that asks the least of us, the way that ensures the *status quo* is disturbed as little as possible. Of course, the easy option need not necessarily be the wrong one, any more than the hard option must always prove right, but, as the Sermon on the Mount makes abundantly clear, more often than not discipleship involves difficult decisions and costly challenges. It means turning the other cheek, loving our enemies, going the extra mile. It involves seeking treasures in heaven rather than treasure on earth. It entails taking the way of the poor in spirit and pure in heart, the meek and merciful, those who are willing, if necessary, to be persecuted for the cause of Christ.

Entering through the narrow gate, then, involves far more than simply committing ourselves to Christ. It means being ready throughout our lives to take difficult decisions that frequently will run counter to the normative values of society. It means having the courage to stand out in the crowd rather than go along with it, to hold firm to our convictions despite the pressure to compromise, to choose the wisdom of God even though it seems folly in the eyes of the world. The temptation to turn back and take the less gruelling path will always be there, beguiling us with the idea that there are various routes to the same goal. It is easy to set off along the narrow way, far harder to continue to the end. Will you be among the handful that succeeds?

Pray

Forgive me, Lord,
    for I took the easy path once again, didn't I?
I didn't mean to,
    or so I tell myself;
    it's just that life was fraught,
    difficult,
    demanding –
    so much to get done,
    so many problems to sort out –
    and so I decided,
    just the once,
    to take the comfortable route,
    the least taxing path,
    promising that next time would be different.
Only that's what I said last time . . .
    and the time before . . .
    and the time before that:
    forever resolving that one day,
    when the moment is right,
    I'll face the challenge,
    walk more faithfully the way of Christ,
    grapple with what it means to carry my cross.
It's not enough, I see that now,
    for the reason the way is narrow is *because* it's hard;
    because following you involves tough decisions,
    awkward choices,
    here and now,
    in all the hurly-burly of life,
    the pressures and responsibilities of the daily routine.
It won't be easier tomorrow or the next day,
    for it's not meant to be –

145

discipleship about costly loving, giving and serving –
and if I keep on ducking the issue until the time is right,
I'll go on doing so for ever,
taking the wide gate by default,
the path that leads to ruin.
Forgive me, Lord,
and, by your grace, help me to change.
Help me, starting from this moment,
when faced by the need to decide,
to choose not the easy way,
but *your* way,
however challenging that might be.
Amen.

Ponder

- When did you last take the path of least resistance? What did you do, and why? What should you have done?
- How will you respond next time something costly is asked of you? Will you be any more ready then than you were last time to respond faithfully?
- What aspects of Christian discipleship do you find most difficult to live by? Have you faced up to the challenge they bring, or do you keep on deferring it? Which way do you take in practice: the narrow or wide way?

Close

Living God,
show me the path I must tread,
guide my footsteps,
and keep me from going astray.
However hard the way,
help me to continue faithfully along it,
walking with perseverance
until I reach my journey's end.
Amen.

Day 36: False prophets

Approach

Living God,
  I would hear your voice,
  your word;
  not mine or any other.
Speak now
  and help me to listen and respond,
  in Jesus' name.
Amen.

Read

Watch out for bogus prophets. Outwardly, they may seem as innocent as sheep, but deep down they are slavering wolves. Their fruits will give them away.
Matthew 7:15-16a

Reflect

'Hello,' said the voice on the other end of the phone line. 'Severiano Ballesteros here.' For a second I hesitated, wondering if it really was the great man himself (I was copy-editing a book at the time on his illustrious career, so it seemed just about possible). But no: the accent was too outrageous and the voice somehow familiar. It was my brother-in-law winding me up, as is his wont. I may have seen through the hoax that time, but on other occasions I've been taken in, hook, line and sinker. You, of course, may be less credulous than me, but few of us are above having the wool pulled over our eyes in the right circumstances.

So who are the false prophets of today? Are there those in the Church who would deliberately lead us astray? I very much doubt it, for if they wanted to do that why would they be in the

Church at all? Are there some who might inadvertently do so? That's more possible, for all of us can be sincere but sincerely wrong. In this modern age, with all kinds of moral and ethical questions relating to modern scientific discovery as to what it means to be human, there is clearly the possibility of well-intentioned but misplaced advice, though it would be a brave or foolhardy person to pronounce unequivocally on who's right and who's wrong. Theological research and other academic disciplines have equally changed our understanding of the world in ways that pose questions of faith; here too there is clearly the possibility of error on both sides. Yet if the threat may come from within, it is probably much more likely to be from closer to home still, and much more innocuous. It's not that another believer would consciously lead us astray – or, at least, I hope not – but we can all succumb to the temptation to water down our faith, to round off the awkward edges, to accommodate the more demanding aspects of discipleship with a less unsettling interpretation of faith, and though we might recognise and resist that temptation in ourselves, when it comes from others, particularly those we respect, it can be hard to resist. If they say it's OK, we reason, then surely it must be. We're clearly being too strict in our understanding.

Yet if these provide some ways of interpreting Jesus' warning concerning bogus prophets, I suspect the greatest threat is likely to come from outside the Church. There are, of course, obvious candidates: pedlars of drugs and pornography; loan-sharks, fraudsters and the like, each all too eager to ensnare the unwary. The image of slavering wolves is well suited to such people, but the dangers they pose are self-evident, and most of us will probably be on our guard against them. More insidious is the culture of which we are a part; a culture that bombards us with images, advertisements, ideas and assumptions that all too easily shape the way we think, slowly but surely conforming us to the way of this world rather than the way of Christ. Without us even being aware of it, the pressure to go along with the crowd is constantly being applied in myriad ways, touching on almost every aspect of life. It's hard to stand up for what we believe when that means standing out in a crowd. It's hard to stand up for justice when we are part of a world structured in favour of the rich and powerful. It's hard to resist the comforts of this world, when the mighty machinery of marketing is geared to making us want more. And so we could go on. The threat here is strongest because it is least obvious. Where temptation is plain it is easier to resist, but when it comes in obscure guises it is hard to recognise, let alone combat. Beware of all that surreptitiously may nibble away at your faith, eroding your convictions, undermining your principles and indiscernibly leading you away from Christ. Whoever you are, the danger is more real than you might think.

Pray

Was I taken in, Lord?
Partly, perhaps,
    a bit of me fooled by the persuasive arguments,
    the attractive, alluring promises.
But much of me,
    deep down,
    wanted to be deceived:
    to hear what I wanted to hear
    and see what I wanted to see.
I was looking for an excuse, I suppose –
    a way of making discipleship a little easier,
    a fraction less demanding,
    for though I talk casually of sacrifice,
    of walking the way of the cross,
    I find the idea daunting;
    surrendering anything is hard enough
    let alone my all.
I'm just too human, that's the truth of it,
    my ways not your ways
    nor my thoughts your thoughts,
    and the tension shows,
    impossible to hide.

149

I yearn to do your will,
    but want *mine* as well.
I hunger for treasure in heaven,
    but thirst equally for riches on earth.
I mean to turn from evil,
    yet can't resist temptation.
I resolve to serve others,
    but end up serving self.
Time and again, Lord, the gulf is exposed,
    and it hurts to face that challenge,
    so I shut it out,
    stopping my ears to whatever might disturb,
    listening instead to a more comfortable gospel,
    accommodated to my needs,
    promising gain without pain,
    all the rewards with none of the cost.
Forgive me, Lord,
    and save me from settling for a peace where there is no peace,
    a life which is no life,
    a 'truth' that is false.
Teach me to listen to your voice,
    however testing your call,
    and to follow where you lead,
    however hard the path,
    for you alone can offer food that satisfies,
    fulfilment that endures,
    hope that shall not fail
    and joy for all eternity.
Receive my praise,
    in the name of Christ.
Amen.

Ponder

- What aspects of discipleship do you find most demanding? Have you succumbed to the temptation to water down the challenge of the gospel?
- Is it possible to be on one's guard against false prophets, yet at the same time not to judge people?
- Are false prophets of today to be found inside or outside the Church?

Close

Living God,
    save me from being led astray
    by those who proclaim what I want to hear,
    teach what I want to believe,
    urge what I want to follow,
    and propound what I find easy to accept.
Open my ears to voices that challenge and disturb,
    trouble and unsettle,
    question and confront –
    to all who speak in your name.
Amen.

Day 37: Good and bad fruits

Approach

Living God,
  grow in me
  so that I may grow in you.
Feed me by your Spirit,
  nurture me through the living presence of Christ,
  and so may I live to your praise and glory.
Amen.

Read

Do you harvest grapes from a briar, or figs from a thistle? To push the analogy, good comes from good trees, and bad from bad. There is no way a good tree can produce bad fruit any more than a bad tree can produce good. Every tree that fails to yield good fruit is felled and hurled into an incinerator. The message, in other words, is this: you can assess people by their fruits.
Matthew 7:16b-20

Reflect

Out in the garden, at the time of writing, I have some gooseberry bushes, and I'm glad to say that these have a decent crop of fruit on them. In fact, I'm looking forward to going out shortly and harvesting some, in readiness for a dish or two of gooseberry crumble. It's all a far cry from a year ago. The bushes then were a pitiable spectacle, covered in thick sticky mildew with barely a fruit in sight. I'd neglected to thin out the branches or clear some space around the plants, and as a result each bush had become diseased. It would have been easy to dig up those plants and throw them away, but thankfully I persevered with them, giving each a bit of tender loving care, and the results are there for all to see, the health of each bush self-evident.

What do people see, I wonder, when they look at you and me? Do they see a spectacle such as those bushes currently present, or a sight more akin to their appearance not so long ago? Do they see, in other words, signs of a healthy flourishing discipleship, or evidence that our relationship with God is not all it should be? You'll all know the sort of fruits we ought to be bearing: the kind of harvest talked about by the Apostle Paul in his letter to the Galatians: 'love, joy, peace, patience, generosity, faithfulness, gentleness and self-control' (5:22). Do those characterise us, or are other fruits more in evidence: bitterness, jealousy, anger, pride, tetchiness, intolerance? According to Jesus, the characteristics we display in our daily lives speak volumes about our discipleship and relationship with him. The harvest we produce may be less than perfect, in all probability a mixture of good and bad fruit, but if there is an excess of the latter over the former, then it cannot but call into question the reality of our commitment. Indeed, if we consistently fail to produce good fruit, producing bad instead, there comes a point when any claim to faith is belied by the facts. It's not, of course, as we have already noted and shall note again in the next session, that faith is dependent on works; rather that certain fruits are a natural consequence of a life lived in relationship to Christ.

Here, it would seem, is the one yardstick by which we may judge others, not condemning or criticising on the basis of some narrow moralistic stance but simply assessing whether their deeds match their words, speaking of Christ or denying him. But before we presume to assess anyone, we do well first to assess ourselves and to ensure that our lives are as firmly rooted in him as we like to imagine.

Pray

It's not much of a harvest, Lord, is it?
Not when you think of the years you've nurtured me,
    the way you've so patiently and lovingly tended my faith,
    seeking to cultivate fruits of your Spirit able to nourish others
        in turn.

153

Not that I've been barren –
   at least that's true –
   occasional deeds of love,
   acts of kindness
   and gestures of compassion
   testimony to your creative touch,
   your life-giving hand at work.
But those have been all too few,
   a mere taste of the rich harvest you yearn to see.
It's not for want of trying, Lord,
   you know that.
If anything, I've tried too hard,
   believing that through sheer willpower I can yield a harvest,
   good intentions enough to produce good fruit.
Forgive me, Lord,
   for I got it wrong,
   imagining *I* can achieve what is down to *you*.
Forgive me for seeing myself as the vine
   rather than simply a branch,
   dependent on you for sustenance, strength and support.
Come now, and promote growth from the fresh shoots of faith.
Prune away whatever is sterile,
   feed what is sound,
   and so may my life blossom anew
   and be truly fruitful,
   to the glory of your name.
Amen.

Ponder

- Are any of the fruits of the Spirit identified by Paul present in your life? Which are not?
- What other fruits of faith do you think God might want to see you producing? How far are these actually present?
- Are you continuing to grow in faith? Is your discipleship as healthy as it should be? Is your life firmly rooted in Christ?

Close

Sovereign God,
    sow within me the seeds of faith,
    truth,
    hope
    and love.
Tend and nurture them through your Spirit,
    nourish them by the grace of Christ,
    and so may my life bear fruit for you,
    a harvest testifying to your redeeming grace
    and renewing power,
    through Jesus Christ my Lord.
Amen.

Day 38: Faith and works

Approach
Loving God,
    teach me not just to believe in you
    but also to live for you,
    so that all I am and do may testify to your love
    and further your kingdom.
Amen.

Read

Not everyone saying to me, 'Lord, Lord' will enter the kingdom of heaven, but only the one who does the will of my heavenly Father. Many will approach me on the last day, arguing, 'Lord, Lord, didn't we utter prophecies, exorcise demons and perform innumerable other deeds of power in your name?' In reply, though, I will tell them, 'Get away from me, you reprobates; I've never known you!'
Matthew 7:21-23

Reflect

Conduct a poll among Christians as to their favourite passage of Scripture and I doubt that our verses today would come anywhere near the Top Ten. Indeed, most of us would probably prefer to forget that Jesus ever uttered these words, for they sit very awkwardly with the message of the gospel as we like to perceive it: that we are justified by faith, not works, salvation given by God's grace alone rather than linked to anything we might do. I wouldn't want to undermine that conviction for a moment, for we are all weak and fallible human beings who repeatedly find ourselves unable to live up to the high calling of Christ. The central message of the good news is indeed that God is always ready to give us a second chance, welcoming us as his children, however little we deserve it. Yet this is not, and never can be, the same as saying that the way we live doesn't matter; that faith can be completely divorced from works, as though the latter is ultimately of no consequence.

As we have seen, Jesus spoke many times during his ministry of the need for Christians to bear fruit; indeed, of the inevitability of us doing just that if our relationship with him is everything it should be. That idea, as we have seen, was taken up and developed by the Apostle Paul in his words concerning the fruits of, or life in, the Spirit. In his parable of the sheep and goats (to be found once again in Matthew), Jesus uncompromisingly set out the importance of actions reinforcing and testifying to the reality of faith, the one inseparable from the other. Most unequivocal of all, we have the Epistle of James, the central tenet of which is that faith without works is dead. The relationship between the two comes down to a simple issue of chronology: works are never a *prerequisite* of faith, but they should always be a *consequence* of it, what we believe and what we have experienced of God's love showing itself in some concrete way. Does that mean, as the words of Jesus seem to suggest, that a failure to exhibit good works puts us beyond his love? The answer, I think, all depends on the reason. If we genuinely aim to offer committed service in word and deed – and I mean *genuinely* – then surely the answer is no, for that would be to deny the efficacy of his grace and mercy. But if we have no intention of living differently – no desire to serve and no hint in our lives of faith translated into action – then it is impossible not to question the validity of our discipleship.

That, I believe, is what Jesus is getting at in these disturbing words of his. He's not suggesting we need to earn his love or merit salvation. Rather, he's urging us to take a long hard look at ourselves and to ask whether the commitment we profess is as real as we might imagine; to ask whether we've understood what discipleship is all about, and whether we've actually made any place for him in our hearts at all. Get that wrong and we may cry out 'Lord, Lord' as often as we like yet find no answering response, still less a welcome, for we will have failed to understand what the word 'Lord', and the person behind it, really means.

Pray

Lord,
　Lord,
　what's happening?
Why don't you answer?
Can't you hear me?
You know who I am, surely:
　your faithful servant,
　committed disciple,
　loyal and devoted follower.
All right,
　perhaps not that faithful, after all,
　nor so committed and loyal as I might be,
　but a servant and disciple nonetheless,
　for didn't I publicly declare my allegiance,
　gladly commit myself to your cause?
Come on, Lord,
　you can't deny it,
　and I don't believe you'd ever want to,
　so what's going on?
Why the stony silence,
　this feeling I'm beating my head against a brick wall?
What's that you say? –
　you don't recognise me,
　don't know who I am!
But you must do!
Come on, think:
　it was me in church last Sunday,
　singing that hymn,
　sharing that prayer,
　offering those gifts.

It was me this morning,
   committing the day to you,
   asking for guidance,
   seeking your blessing.
You *can't* have forgotten.
What do you mean, *I* forgot *you* –
   failing to hear your call in the cry of my neighbour:
   the groans of the hungry,
   the plight of the weak,
   the despair of the sick,
   the pain of the lonely?
Why didn't you tell me it was you?
That's all it needed.
I'd have helped then, of course I would.
But I was in a rush to get home,
   short of loose change,
   snowed under with work,
   late for church –
   you know the sort of thing.
I never meant to shut you out,
   still less let you down.
Come on, Lord,
   be reasonable;
   you must understand.
You do, don't you?
Lord . . . ?

Ponder

- Does your faith show itself in action?
- Do you sometimes subconsciously use the idea of justification by faith alone to justify a failure to show faith in action?
- Are you guilty sometimes of allowing religious observance to become more important than practical service?

Close

Gracious God,
    may I not simply proclaim you as Lord,
    nor simply worship you as such,
    but also live each day to your glory,
    showing the sincerity of my commitment
    through the depth of my love,
    the extent of my service
    and the pattern of my life,
    to the glory of your name.
Amen.

Day 39: A firm foundation

Approach

Sovereign God,
  teach me as I read your word
  to understand it
  and apply it,
  so that, come what may, my faith may be strong
  and my commitment sure.
Amen.

Read

Whoever hears my words and acts on them will be like someone who wisely constructed a house on an outcrop of rock. When the rain poured down, floodwaters rose and gales battered that house, it did not collapse, because its foundations were on rock. On the other hand, to hear my words and fail to apply them is akin to the fool who built his house on sand. When this time the rain poured down, floodwaters rose and gales battered that house, it collapsed – and what a mighty crash it was!
Matthew 7:24-27

Reflect

What must we do in order to build our lives upon rock? 'That's easy!' we may say. 'Base our lives upon the gospel. Put our trust in Christ. Commit our lives to him in faith.' Well, perhaps, but is that actually what Jesus says? Take another look at the parable of the wise and foolish builders, and at the interpretation Jesus gives of it, and I think you'll find it's not quite so simple. No doubt, he would be encouraged by a response such as I've outlined, but, at least as I read it, he is saying slightly more. Wisdom, he says, consists in hearing 'these words of mine' and building one's life

161

upon them. In other words, he's not talking here of the gospel as such, vital though that is. He's referring specifically to the teaching given in the Sermon on the Mount; in other words, to the diverse challenges, instructions, sayings and ideas that we've focused on throughout this book. That's not to say, of course, that discipleship is dependent on obeying all of these to the letter; that would be to succumb to just the sort of legalism that Jesus was so intent on countering. It is not to claim that faith can be reduced to certain good works; that would be to deny the purpose of his suffering and death. Jesus, though, isn't talking here of salvation; rather, he's setting out what is needed to give our discipleship firm foundations, the sort of things we ought to focus on if we hope to grow as Christians. If we don't put these words into practice, he will not discard or reject us; his love and grace goes on being as real as always. What we may find, however, is that our commitment grows cold and our love wanes as, imperceptibly but inexorably, our love becomes detached from the daily business of living.

So what do you make of these words of Jesus, of this extraordinarily powerful body of teaching? Have you nodded sagely and then forgotten to think further? Have you resolved to live differently only to lose sight of that promise? Have you applauded the sentiments, yet decided the words do not apply to you? Or have you reflected, understood, and then prayed for help to apply what Jesus has to say to the life you live and the person you are? If so, you are ready to face whatever life might bring and to stand firm despite it all. If not, however real your faith and strong your commitment, you may find that your discipleship, the very foundations upon which you have built your life, are not as secure as you like to assume.

Pray

I'm no fool, Lord, that's for sure.
I may have my faults,
    but I've built my life upon Christ,
    the chief cornerstone,
    the rock upon which all else rests.
No danger, then, of my faith falling,
    my commitment starting to crumble,
    for I've done all I need to do, surely –
    made the decision that shapes everything,
    holds all of life together.
At least that's what I thought,
    until I read these words of yours –
    truly read them –
    and suddenly I'm less sure of my ground,
    for they unsettle,
    trouble,
    disturb,
    portraying someone else, not me:
    a quality of discipleship I rarely if ever attain;
    a depth of wisdom, love and dedication that I often aspire to
    yet get nowhere near.
I realise that your love sets no conditions –
    that salvation is down to your grace rather than my goodness –
    but you must at least hope for results,
    something to show that I've changed,
    that I'm serious about loving you in return –
    and even if *you* can live without that,
    I can't,
    for if I fail to make you part of me –
    putting your word into practice
    and honouring your will –
    then it's only a matter of time, I fear,
    before I drift away,
    my relationship with you becoming more apparent than real.
So help me, Lord, truly to base my life on you;

to build each day on firm foundations,
solid rock.
It's not easy, I know that,
requiring patience, effort, determination,
but you've given me the bricks and mortar,
and shown me what needs doing.
Now help me to build!
Amen.

Ponder

- How much of Jesus' teaching in the Sermon on the Mount, if any, can you truthfully claim to have put into practice in your life?
- Which words do you find hardest to act on? Why?
- How important do you think it is to base your life on such teaching?

Close

Almighty God,
teach me to build my life on the rock of faith,
the foundations of truth
and the cornerstone of Christ,
each part cemented together by love.
So, through good or bad,
joy or sorrow,
pleasure or pain,
may I stand firm,
secure in the knowledge of your sovereign purpose
and saving grace.
Amen.

Day 40: The ultimate authority

Approach

Loving God,
   help me to read your word not as an academic exercise,
   nor in a casual cursory fashion,
   but hearing your voice addressing my mind,
   my heart,
   my soul –
   my life in every part.
Speak now,
   speak always,
   in the name of Christ.
Amen.

Read

The crowd, having heard Jesus out to the end, were dumbfounded at his teaching, for he spoke with an aura of natural authority, quite unlike anything they had heard from their scribes.
Matthew 7:28

Reflect

Why base our lives on the words of Jesus? Because we read them in the Bible? Some might suggest so, but in reality that is simply to rephrase the question, for why base our lives on the Bible? The reason Matthew gives for listening to Jesus is far more specific, and worth reflecting on in terms of Scripture as a whole. 'What sort of teacher and what sort of teaching is this?' was the question on everyone's lips after listening to Jesus' words, for here was someone who carried an aura of credibility quite different to anything they discerned among their own experts in religion and the law. What was so different? He spoke, we are told, with authority.

165

But what does that mean? What was it specifically about the things Jesus said and the way he said them that made such a profound impression. Perhaps partly it was the unequivocal, even dogmatic, nature of his teaching: 'You have heard it was said . . .' he repeatedly stated, 'but I say to you . . .' There was no trace here of the laborious qualifications of the scribes and Pharisees, no dotting the i's and crossing the t's. Instead, he laid things on the line, straight down the middle, no punches pulled. Undoubtedly, this directness added to Jesus' charisma, yet we should beware of pushing it too far, for what can be a virtue can also be a vice, many a reactionary and doctrinaire orator having spoken with equal candour. Surely what set Jesus apart was the fact that his words rang true, getting under people's skin in the sense that no one could evade the challenge he brought to their lifestyles, attitudes and actions. Some eventually might have chosen to reject what he said, just as many do today, but none could fail to be made at least to think. For the multitudes drawn to Jesus, here was someone whose words linked the ordinary with the heavenly, the mundane with the divine, making God relevant to the humdrum routine of life.

What of you? No one can force you to accept Jesus' words as seminal for your life, and hopefully no one would want to – certainly not Jesus. But can you honestly say, having read and reflected upon them, that they have failed to touch you, not simply superficially but at a far more significant level deep within? If they've left you unmoved, then no one can blame you if you decide to dismiss them without a second thought. But, if like the listeners to the Sermon on the Mount long ago, they've quickened your conscience, stirred your imagination, questioned your way of life and nourished your spirit, then, quite honestly, what more authority do you need to act upon them? Isn't it time to stop wavering and to start following this blueprint for life?

Pray

Lord,
    there are so many voices clamouring for my attention,
    so many people telling me how to run my life –
    books and newspapers,
    radio and television,
    family and friends,
    folk in the Church,
    each offering words, words, words.
They mean well, no doubt –
    well, most of them, anyway –
    and I need what they offer,
    for my knowledge is partial,
    my understanding limited,
    my horizons flawed.
I can't go it alone
    and I wouldn't want to,
    the insights of others vital to complement my own,
    their advice, influence and guidance a healthy balance
    to my errors and weaknesses,
    but they can only offer signposts,
    not provide the way;
    at best afford glimpses of reality,
    not embody truth itself;
    the most any can offer just a window on to life
    rather than life in all its fullness.
Your word, Lord, is different:
    simple, yet profound,
    disturbing, yet full of promise,
    revealing my emptiness, yet filling to overflowing,
    exposing all that is wrong within me, yet bringing inner healing.
I struggle to understand sometimes –
    so much in life troubling and confusing –
    but you speak like none other,
    touching the very soul,
    and though I might resist,

evade,
you go on calling,
questioning,
confronting.
How can I do anything but respond?
Amen.

Ponder

- How far does the teaching of Jesus strike you as carrying authority? In what way?
- What aspects of Jesus' teaching particularly speak to and challenge you?
- How far do you live as though the words of Jesus carry authority in your life? Is it time you attempted more seriously to live up to them?

Close

Lord Jesus Christ,
    teach me to hear your voice
    and to respond to your challenging word,
    recognising that what you say has authority over my life
    and over all;
    a voice unlike any other,
    speaking the word of life.
In your name I pray.
Amen.